The Tibetan Medicine and Your Health

Dr. Lobsang Wangyal checking the pulse of His Holiness the Dalai Lama.

The Tibetan Medicine *and* Your Health

Tove Langemyr Larsen

MOTILAL BANARSIDASS PUBLISHERS
PRIVATE LIMITED • DELHI

Reprint: Delhi, 2014
First Edition: Delhi, 2011

ISBN: 978-81-208-3445-3 (Paper)

MOTILAL BANARSIDASS

41 U.A. Bungalow Road, Jawahar Nagar, Delhi 110 007
8 Mahalaxmi Chamber, 22 Bhulabhai Desai Road, Mumbai 400 026
203 Royapettah High Road, Mylapore, Chennai 600 004
236, 9th Main III Block, Jayanagar, Bengaluru 560 011
Sanas Plaza, 1302 Baji Rao Road, Pune 411 002
8 Camac Street, Kolkata 700 017
Ashok Rajpath, Patna 800 004
Chowk, Varanasi 221 001

Printed in India

by RP Jain at NAB Printing Unit
A-44, Naraina Industrial Area, Phase I, New Delhi–110028
and published by JP Jain for Motilal Banarsidass Publishers (P) Ltd
41 U.A. Bungalow Road, Jawahar Nagar, Delhi-110007

THE DALAI LAMA

MESSAGE

Tibetan medicine is one of the greatest legacies of Tibetan Buddhist civilization. It is a system that can contribute substantially to maintaining a healthy mind and a healthy body. Like the traditional Indian and Chinese systems, Tibetan medicine views health as a question of balance. A variety of circumstances such as diet, lifestyle, seasonal and mental conditions can disturb this natural balance, which gives rise to different kinds of disorders.

As an integrated system of health care Tibetan medicine has served the Tibetan people well for many centuries and I believe can still provide much benefit to humanity at large. The difficulty we face in bringing this about is one of communication, for, like other scientific systems, Tibetan medicine must be understood in its own terms, as well as in the context of objective investigation.

This book is a compilation of articles and talks by qualified Tibetan physicians and scholars of Tibetan medicine, who in addition to their traditional training in Tibet and India have been exposed to a modern scientific environment. Therefore, I am confident that it will be of great benefit to serious students of Tibetan medicine, as well as providing an opportunity for general readers to appreciate this valuable but sometimes overlooked aspect of the Tibetan cultural heritage.

༄༅། །བོད་གཞུང་སྨན་རྩིས་ཁང་།

MEN - TSEE - KHANG

Tel. : *0091-1892-307068/307069/223222*
Fax : *0091-1892-224116*
E-mail : *tmai@men-tsee-khang.org*
tmai@vsnl.com
Website : *www.men-tsee-khang.org*

(Tibetan Medical & Astrological Institute of H.H. the Dalai Lama)
Gangchen Kyishong, Dharamsala - 176 215, H.P., INDIA

MESSAGE

Mrs. Tove Langemyr Larsen is a very close friend of Men-Tsee-Khang, striving hard in promoting our unique system of healing in Norway. From 1985 to 1998, she hosted and organized our doctor's visit to Norway which had been very successful. She has also worked very hard in other important projects for the cause of Tibet and its people. In 1999, she had to withdraw from hosting the tour due to her old age and other genuine problems.

This book on Tibetan Medicine she is bringing out, is a compilation of articles and talks given by senior Tibetan physicians and scholars, and will surely help many enthusiastic foreigners to open up their eyes to the world of Tibetan Medicine.

I would like to express my sincere thanks to Mrs. Tove Langemyr Larsen for working very hard in bringing up this book and also to her husband for supporting her, which would help in the promotion and propagation of Tibetan Medicine for the humanity at large.

May all sentient being live in peace, harmony & healthy !

Dr. Tsewang Tamdin
Director
Men-Tsee-Khang
Dated: April 14, 2010

A Society registered under the Societies Registration Act XXI of 1860.

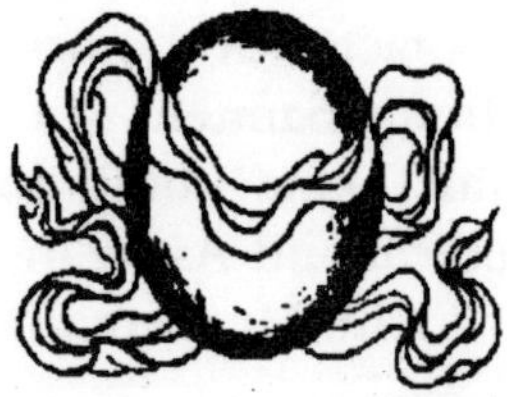

The pearl entwined with a scarf is a symbol of good angury.

ACKNOWLEDGEMENTS

The warmest thanks goes to the late Dr. Lobsang Wangyal, the personal physician of H.H. the Dalai Lama. I also humbly acknowledge the useful contributions of following Tibetan doctors (for brief bio of these doctors please see Appendix III, pp. 197-200) on various topics – Lobsang Wangyal *(Balance of tempremements, Digestion, Treatments, Hormany theraphy, High blood pressure, Multiple sclerosis, Tibetan psychiatry)* Namgyal Qusar (*Digestion, Skin diseases*), Dawa (*Heart diseases*), Lobsang Rapgay (*Urine diagnosis, Cancer*), Lobsang Tsultrim Tsona (*Cupping and moxa acupuncture, Goldhammer treatment, arthrosis and arthritis*), Tsewang Tamdim (*Headaches, Asthma, Vitiligo*), Pema Dorjee (*Rheumatism*), Dorjee Rapten Neshar (*Heart diseases*), Namgyal Tenzin (*Skin diseases*), Tenzin Choedak (*Diabetes, AIDS*), Thokmay Paljor and all the other. I do not claim to be the real author of this book, I have only adapted, commented and added many case stories which I was priviledged to know during the consultations with these doctors.

I am also deeply grateful to H.H. the Dalai Lama, for the message he has written for this book – his heart is very strongly with Tibetan medicine.

Thanks also to his religious assistant, reverend Lhakdor, now director of Tibetan Museum and Archives, who accompanied Dr. Wangyal as interpreter during his first visit to Norway. Hearty thanks also to my friend Thubten, who got the ball rolling, to H.H. the Dalai Lama's representative, Phuntzog Wangyal, in London at the time we started, who in turn put me in contact with the brother of His Holiness the Dalai Lama, Lobsang Samten, who sadly died abruptly, his wife Mrs. Namgyal Taklha – both directors of Men-Tsee-Khang (Tibetan Medical and Astro Institute) in exile, and the directors Mr. T. Tashi, Mr. Pema Dadhul Arya, and Dr. Dawa.

In addition, I express my thanks to Dr. Vilhelm Schjelderup, Berit Falch, and Anne Harila, Hans B. Butenschoen and my Norwegian publisher, Roald Pettersen.

Illustrations: Thanks to late Hallvard Kåre Kuløy, for permitting me to use the illustrations from his book on Tibetan carpets, to Dr. Dawa and Men-Tsee-Khang for illustrations and drawings, and to Wisdom Publications. Warm thank also to all my other helpers in Men-Tsee-Khang.

Warm thanks to my dear husband Gunnar and son and electronics engineer Tore, for their untiring support. And to Anna Richard, who so willingly corrected my English.

The peony: The flower of spring

CONTENTS

Appendices

Clouds as used in Tibetan carpets

PREFACE

Nearly 33 years ago I was operated on for cancer in the ovaries. After the operation I felt fit as a fiddle, but the doctors said I needed a second hysterectomy in six weeks' time, to remove a bit more, and fill the abdomen with radioactive liquid gold. That was the end of the fitness. The result was paralysis in the digestive system, and insistent diarrhoea. I was told to live on Nestlé's five-months baby food, for the rest of my life. The doctors gave me five years to live. On leaving the hospital, I never touched it, too stubborn, and too determined to try anything else.

To add to the misery, I also received chemotherapy. Fortunately, the doctor was a bit confused about the time allotted. He had prescribed six months chemo, but had obviously forgotten that, when I told him he had prescribed only three months.

Just as I got home, my husband, at that time a personnel manager, hired a new doctor for his firm. This doctor proved to be a pioneer at the time, practicing reflexology for diagnosis, then homeopathy and acupuncture. His wife ran courses on vegetarian diet.

Over the next few years I tried about everything there was in alternative medicine, and got some benefit here and there.

Thubten's Dream: Then one day, our Tibetan friend Thubten exclaimed – "You, who have experienced so many alternative therapies, you should try Tibetan medicine. It has for a long time been my dream to get a Tibetan doctor to visit Norway." Even before explaining what Tibetan medicine was all about, I felt this was important – "Let's do it, Thubten!"

So Thubten wrote to the Dalai Lama's brother, whom he knew, and who was then the director of the Tibetan Medical Institute in exile, in Dharamsala in the north India, where the Dalai Lama lives.

That was the beginning. The Dalai Lama's personal physician, Dr. Lobsang Wangyal*, came with an interpreter, as he spoke Tibetan only. They both charmed us all, with their knowledge and deep compassion. With their radiant smiles and their humour.

At first the consultations were carried out in Thubten's home. His wife Lobsang, an assistant nurse, got leave from her job to conduct it all – with two doctors living in the flat, patients flocking to see the doctor, Lobsang interpreting into Norwegian. However, there was one who did not appreciate this at all – her four year old Norbo! Usually my husband and I were drowned in hugs from this happy boy, but in those two weeks he ignored us completely. Poor kid – a rush of foreign people and intensely busy parents, was just a bit too much. But slowely he adjusted and by the time two weeks had passed, he was again the same happy, hugging little lad.

For the next ten years, Dr. Wangyal, 'Amchi-la' as we called him (*amchi* means doctor in Tibetan), kept visiting Norway each September, along with a young Tibetan doctor as an assistant and interpreter – all of them possessing the same quality, warm radiant smiles from the depth of their soul, deep compassion and joyous humour. Daily, patients commented that their meeting with Amchi-la and his young assistants were a great experience.

---

* For details see Appendix III

I will never forget one young man – he wept after the consultation, wept with relief and joy! After a long time, a doctor believed in him, and who diagnosed what was wrong. Earlier Norwegian doctors diagnosed his ailments as psychological, even when he bled from his ears. However, Amchi-la explained, "you have been poisoned and that has harmed your liver and heart." Actually, as a small child he had fallen into a sewage container, and by the time his brother pulled him out, he had swallowed a great deal of sewage.

Many patients enquired us, whether there was anything they could do for the exiled Tibetans. This resulted in setting up of a small humanitarian society – "Friends of Tibet." Some friends also sponsored school children and medical students, others brought money or clothes. The society imported hand-made Tibetan carpets, the income supported a school building, a refugee centre and small houses for elderly people, among other things.

Thubten's dream has come true, more than he ever expected, and with the formation of "Friends of Tibet." The doctors' visits continue, Thubten's dream lives on.

The endless knot: Love and compassion

INTRODUCTION

Tibetan medicine is about 2500 years old. And some of its elements are even older, about 5000 years or more.

In the seventh century it made a big leap forward when, the then thousand year old, Indian Ayurvedic medicine was at its height. The personal physician of Tibetan king, Ṭrisong Detsen, travelled to India and brought the knowledge of the Ayurvedic medicine back to Tibet. Here it was combined with the existing Tibetan medical practice.

Trisong's grandson Yuthok Younten Gonpo, who was in his time also the personal physician of the Tibetan king, travelled to India three times to pick up more knowledge. With that, Tibetan medicine really started to flourish. Perhaps, Yuthok's own life was proof of the benefits of the now fully-grown Tibetan medicine, as he lived to the ripe old age of 125 years.

During the following centuries the Ayurvedic medicine began to decline in India. Much was forgotten during that period, but it was luckily preserved in Tibet. Not only preserved, but also enriched with influences from China, Nepal and Persia. In the eighth century Tibet had its first international medical symposium, with leading Indian, Chinese, Nepalese doctors, plus a Persian doctor. This Persian doctor stayed on in Tibet for quite a while. Persian medicine was also strongly influenced by Greek medicine and philosophy, and parts of this influence is to this day easily recognizable in Tibetan medicine, when you read about the temperaments, and the urine diagnosis.

In the ninth century the first book on Tibetan psychiatry was written – the first book ever on psychiatry, I wonder? There are for instance descriptions of ailments resembling bulimia and anorexia nervosa!

Some years ago, H.H. the Dalai Lama attended a symposium in the US, which included Western psychologists and psychiatrists. During that symposium the Dalai Lama explained about Tibetan psychiatry. The surprised Western specialists exclaimed – and we thought we had invented psychology, some 200 years ago!

Chinese medicine was greatly influenced by Tibetan medicine, and when Mao more or less quenched the knowledge of acupuncture in China, it was preserved in Tibet.

The teachings of Buddha are strongly present in Tibetan medicine, but then Buddhism is not a theological, but a psychological religion. The very essence of these teachings is that the mind is where all the phenomena start. The mind is the source for stable health, and when out of balance, for illness. Recognize it? It is a fundamental psychosomatic interpretation!

Compare this with Western medicine, as you read on. Western medicine alleges that it is the only valid medicine, because it is based on scientific research and control. What about 2500 years' experience, isn't that profound research? And as you will notice, in Tibetan Medicine the patient is treated as an individual. What is the right medicine for one is not the right medicine for another. We are all different. Tibetan medicine does not treat the symptoms; it follows a guideline for the diagnosis.

What is important is the *cause.* The Tibetan doctor has a different approach to the cause, because the patients have different temperaments. So two patients with the same disease will get different medicines, in relation to which temperaments (defects) are involved.

Tibetan doctors by no means dismiss Western medicine. We need each other, they say, and praise Western medicine for its solution on acute problems, while chronic diseases are better helped through Tibetan medicine.

Tibetan medicine is divided into three groups: *Dharma, tantra* and *somatic medicine.* The theme of this book is the somatic medicine.

Just a few words on the two others: Dharma *medicine uses* spiritual and psychological methods – we would compare such a doctor as a mixture of a priest and a psychiatrist.

They aim to make the patient understand the nature of the mind, so that they can control negative feelings. Meditation is one of the important measures.

The tantric (yogic) medicine covers the part between the mental and the physical, and aims at changing subtle vital energies. These are the same energies which we in the West stimulate through faith, positive thinking and also through the placebo effect.

A fascinating part of harmonizing these subtle energies is through treatment with *Singing bowls.* This kind of treatment has become quite popular among some Western practitioners.

The Singing bowls, and small cymbals and bells, are made of traditionally seven different metals: Gold, mercury, iron, lead, silver, copper and tin. The content of each metal varies in the different sizes of bowls. Every metal manifests its individual sound and harmony – each having its individual medical effect. The sounds that are produced have specific overtones, and when the sound is produced it vibrates for an exceptionally long time.

These are bowls of different sizes in a set, and they are used to balance different vibratory levels in the body. For instance, the sound of the largest Singing bowl placed on or near the abdomen or chest is transmitted, via the skeletal system through the entire body.

Western researchers have found that the sounds influence the body cells, through the liquid in the cells. After all, our bodies consist of 60-65% liquid! A French investigation even found that one specific sound would split up cancerous cells, without affecting the healthy cells. This investigation, though, was not based on the Singing bowls.

In Asia the sound, with overtones used to cure, dates back 3000 years.

My own experience convinced me – After a period, when I was feeling stressed. I received one treatment with the small cymbals, sounding close to my head. It felt as if my brain was being re-shuffled! It was very relaxing, and it lasted too. As long as I did not fill up my brain with another heavy load of stress!

The bat is a symbol much used in Tibetan carpets. In China it is a symbol of good fortune.

Ritual bell

WHAT THE FACE TELLS

The eyes are the flowers of the liver,
The nose is the flower of the lungs,
The ears are the flowers of the kidneys,
The lips are the flowers of the spleen,
The tongue is the flower of the heart.

The eyes represent Fire (bile bladder, liver). If the liver becomes too hot, the whites of the eyes turn yellow. Satisfying Phlegm that cools down the Fire adjusts balanced eye flame.

The nose: When it runs, there is too much brain Phlegm – the snow on the mountain melts.

The ears: When the skin on the ears is humid, or when you have tinnitus – it is related to the kidneys.

The lips: Spleen problems are shown through a hanging lower lip, sores on the lips or when the lips are pink or coated.

The heart: A cracked or dry tongue, indicate heart problems or stuttering, likewise, when, at times the tongue is dark coloured.

Dr. Pema Dorjee*

* For details see Appendix III

The interlocked rings symbolize the queen's earrings.

Chapter - I

BALANCE OF TEMPERAMENTS

If you are in balance, the body can help to heal itself. To restore balance is the key to the diverse alternative types of medicine. I think this is part of what irritates Western doctors. But balance goes deep. You may get some balance on the surface, but for chronic diseases that is just the beginning. There are layers of balance to dig into. It is like peeling an onion. When you have peeled off the first layer, you go on to the next. And each layer needs different medicines. At the beginning it may seem easy to peel the layer because you do feel better. But don't kid yourself, chronic diseases mean that miracles take time. Though from time to time we have registered some surprisingly quick miracles too.

The first thing the Tibetan doctor asks you about is your diet. And amazingly enough, these miracles may come fast: That is, if there is something you eat or drink which works like poison in your body. Dropping these items can result in the quick miracle. That is if you have a craving for a certain food; that may be your one and only enemy!

> JANE was very fat, and her addiction was chocolate and cakes - well, anything sweet. She had tried slimming cures - one after another, lost a few kilos, then regained, and even

increased. The kilos continued to build up. The reason for her sweet tooth was actually nervousness, which was an after effect from a head injury suffered as a child. The head injury had also made her slightly retarded. Sweet tasting food calmed her. But alas, each time the calm effect lasted ever less, and more chocolates and cakes were consumed. The Tibetan doctor explained convincingly, and also gave her gold hammer (see p. 109) acupuncture, to reduce the nervousness and after effects of the old head injury. With some initial medicines added she soon accepted her problem, dropped the sweet stuff, and the many extra kilos disappeared.

ROB was a Western doctor. His wife had psoriasis, and her face looked really ugly. Within less than a year, the Tibetan medicines cured her. Meanwhile complacent Dr. Rob had developed an explosive temperament. He felt so unhappy and desperate that he agreed to see Dr. Wangyal, too. Dr. Wangyal read the pulses on his wrists and studied his urine sample (the Tibetan way), then asked with a smile – "You are fond of strong spices"? Rob, surprised, could only confirm. That is your problem, Dr. Wangyal told him – "Drop the hot spices, and alcohol too. Your health has become too hot, so hot that you explode. Remove everything hot, and you will soon be back to your normal self, without medicines." And that was exactly what happened. A quick miracle!

There are stacks of examples like this, and you will meet more further. Let me just add one more:

JULIA was swimming in fat, a liquid, soft type of fat. She was also so nervous that she had heart trouble. She became very angry when her Western doctor told her that the source of her problems was nervousness. Nonsense!! The Tibetan doctor found that in addition to her nervousness, which was the cause of her heart trouble, her overweight was due to a great fancy for tomatoes. Daily loads of tomatoes. But she was not willing to listen, not willing to take any Tibetan medicine. Her reaction was the same as before: Nonsense!! She is still swimming in fat.

If you are ill, and have a craving, acknowledge it! It is not only alcohol one may become addicted to. Acknowledging your addiction, you may experience your own miracle, be your own doctor. Be aware that stopping consumption of your craving may also give you withdrawal symptoms, even from dropping tomatoes, like an alcoholic or drug addict when they stop their intakes.

The leaf of artemisia symbolises dignity.

The Three Defects

Everyone has heard about yin and yang. In Tibetan somatic medicine this can be explained as "hot" and "cold". But then Tibetan medicine goes deeper, and explains that the body also is dependent on harmony between the three humours, as they call them. Those three humours: Wind, Bile and Phlegm, are expressed as temperaments you are born with. They are expressed as defects when there is imbalances in the body.

The temperaments are thus the inherent characteristics of a person's mind and physical body. But not only you have this kind of inherent characteristic, all food items, and herbal medicines have it too.

The craze Rob had developed was due to the hot characteristics of the hot spices, throwing him out of balance, resulting in a hot defect. Alcohol is hot too. Julia's problem was the tomato, which has a cold and very liquid character. This results in the defects.

The defects are explained as poisons, basically mental poisons – it all starts in your mind. The three temperaments, and the three defects, are of Wind, Bile and Phlegm. The root of the defects is a real basic ignorance, a kind of ignorance all of us possess. That is part of life, we are none of us enlightened, but are "like birds that fly high in the sky and enjoy it, but cannot free themselves from the shadow cast on the ground". Which means that no matter how much we are blessed with good health and happiness, we are not free from the source of suffering, or the risk of falling ill. We are linked to this life.

The three defects, or mental poisons if you like, are:
Desire, which causes **Wind,**
Hatred, which causes **Bile,** and
Delusion, which causes **Phlegm.**

When any of them are out of balance, they are at the root of our problems. (In Tibetan these three defects are called *rLoong, Tripa* and *Badkan,* and if you know anything about Ayurvedic medicine, there they are called *Vata, Pitta* and *Kapha.*)

To help you understand this, and before explaining it more, here is a story:

> DAN was Jane's younger brother. They were neighbours, Dan's house by the main road, Jane's up a steep road behind it. Her road passed over the corner of Dan's site. He was not at all happy about that, but Jane owned this part, which was duly registered in her name as the only access to her house. Jane returned, after having been away for a couple of days, to find the access to her house blocked by no less than three caravans. She first knocked on Dan's door, but no one answered. A thin man in the first caravan (Mr. Wind) shouted and waved his arms – "They will not be back till tomorrow." Jane approached him and said calmly – "Sorry, but you are not allowed to park here. None of you are. This is my private land and you block the access to my house."
>
> The man laughed out loud: "I have paid my rent to the owner, and will not budge", pointing to Dan's house. Jane, still calm – "Sorry, but you have been misled. I am the owner of this part. And this goes for all three of you". The man shouted to the other caravan owners, who joined him, and he volubly told his version of what was happening, eagerly gesturing with a bandaged hand.

The couple in the second caravan (Mr. and Mrs. Phlegm), both well fed, looked questioningly at Jane, who once more tried to explain, but was constantly interrupted by Mr. Wind. This couple were obviously concerned, nodded and prepared to move their caravan.

The third man, (Mr. Bile) with a yellowish skin, a near empty gin bottle in his hand, exploded, red in his head with anger, and with alcohol. He shouted obscenities at Jane, who still remained calm. She picked up her mobile – "Well, if you don't move from here, I will have to call the police here and now". The first man squabbled, the words poured from his mouth. The third man threw more abuse at her, then his bottle. Jane ducked, and the bottle crashed on a stone.

Mr. Wind had a Wind temperament, the words "blowing" out of his mouth, before he even tried to think. He was quick in all his movements, waving his arms as he talked, not standing still. His brain was overactive. He was thin and agile. Regarding his bandaged hand, Wind persons are accident prone, too, because of their hectic behaviour. Being over energetic, he may also become fanatic. Had he been in balance, you would find such a Wind person fond of music, of singing and dancing.

Mrs. and Mr. Phlegm kept calm, accepted the fact. They were sedate in their movements, and fairly fat, with no protruding bones, obviously fond of food, much food. When Mr. Bile threw the bottle, they tried to mediate, but this only made him even angrier. A Phlegm person hates exercise, is complacent, and is a typical mediator. If he can abstain from over eating, and exercise more, he will normally live longer than the Wind and the Bile person.

Mr. Bile had a Bile temperament. Bile is hot and he sweats easily. When out of balance, words are harsh, temperament violent, red hot. Alcohol stimulates the heat, and the violent reactions can turn dangerous. In addition to alcohol, the Bile man loved hot spices, which again fired his heated temperament. And his words hurt, as he was an intelligent man and knew how to attack.

Well, many of us do not have such clear-cut personalities as these caravan owners. We may be a mixture of two or of all three temperaments. Jane's brother Dan was a mixture of Wind and Bile, scheming, then fleeing from trouble, jealous and, resentful. Jane was a very balanced mixture of all three: Wind, Phlegm and Bile.

When the temperaments are not balanced, illness appears. Illness of Wind, illness of Bile and illness of Phlegm, or combinations among the three: Wind+Bile, Wind+Phlegm, Phlegm+Bile, or all three combined. In all there are seven possibilities.

When the temperaments are out of balance then, and become imbalances and illness, these imbalances are the defects.

Actually, there is still another combination which may be linked to any of the seven varieties above, and that is Blood.

Diagnosing this is certainly not easy, if you are not a Tibetan doctor! One of the main defects is usually prevalent though.

You are born with your temperament. A person's nature remains the same throughout one's lifetime. But sometimes, with overindulgence in any characteristic for a very long time, that could even change one's nature. This overindulgence may not only be due to a food craze, but also to wrong lifestyle and behaviour.

Rather inaccurately and superficially we can say that:

Wind resembles the Greek sanguine temperament.

Bile resembles the Greek choleric temperament.

Phlegm resembles the phlegmatic temperament.

I don't know whether this influence started with Greece, or the opposite way – from Tibetan or Ayurvedic philosophy. The Persian doctor who came to Tibet may be a precedent of the communication East-West and West-East, along the caravan routes – the "Silk road", as it was called.

In addition to sorting out your temperament, and the defects, the Tibetan doctor also registers another inborn characteristic of the person: Feminine, masculine and neutral, quite independent of the person being male or female! The doctor uses all his diagnostic possibilities to find out this – studying the person, his body, how he talks and moves, the colour of his skin, studying his tongue, questioning the patient, feeling his twelve pulses, and studying his urine sample – the Tibetan urine analysis is very unique.

Quite a puzzle! No wonder it takes a Tibetan doctor seven years to qualify as a doctor – with five years' theoretical study and two years apprenticeship with a senior doctor. Before 1959, that is before China occupied Tibet, the study lasted twelve years.

To become a good Tibetan doctor you need not only to be intelligent and have a thorough knowledge of medicine, but also to be compassionate, stand by your word, be dedicated and good at social etiquette. Compassion is very essential, and very much part of the Tibetan way of life. The Dalai Lama always stresses how important compassion is.

By the way, it is said that the Chinese doctors in natural medicine and acupuncture do not get paid until the patient has become better or is cured, and get no pay if the patient gets worse or dies. Well, if that rule is true, it can certainly be taken in two ways. If the Chinese doctor does not have the qualities essential to the Tibetan doctors, he might not tend to the patient, who is too ill, in his view, to pay him!

Stylised sky design in Tibetan carpets.

The Three Humours

Wind (*Vata* in Ayurvedic medicine) is a force, a pressure, and the energy that is responsible for *all* the movements and functions in the body.

The thoughts – that is the movements in the brain, movement of muscles through the central and peripheral nervous system, the breathing process, synthesis of bodily essence, the heartbeat and the circulation of the blood, the expansion and contraction in the organs, and the excretion of faeces and urine.

Wind is developed by greed and is directly connected to the mind. It is involved in many illnesses, and also in:

Neuroses and psychoses,

Quickness,

Nervousness,

Fear,

Anxiety,

Worries,

Pain,

Cramps and

Shivering.

Mr. Wind had an overactive brain, so much Wind that it stormed!

Is this you?

The Wind person is skinny and bent, and has a bluish skin colour. He may not be very down to earth. He reacts and works quickly, is enthusiastic and lively, but when out of balance his enthusiasm may become fanatic. He walks quickly, with a light step, a crackling noise may be heard when he moves. He is sensitive to cold and wind.

He is emotional, and may change mood suddenly. He may have difficulty taking decisions, changes his mind quickly, and worries easily.

Learns new things fast, but is not so good at remembering what he has read.

Talks a great deal, speaks fast and effusive.

Sleeps lightly and restlessly, and eats too much or too little at meals. Prefers sweet, sour, bitter and hot tasting food.

He likes singing, laughing, gambling and games.

The Wind person has a short body stature, is usually not blessed with the best health, and may have a shorter life span, compared to the Bile and especially to the Phlegm person. Wind is more dominant when you get older. Phlegm is most dominant in childhood, and Bile during youth. It is typical among the elderly to feel cold.

The Wind person needs heat, warm food, warm clothes (wool), a warm climate and warm colours such as red, orange and yellow. Soups, being warm and liquid, are excellent.

He also needs warm and loving companions.

Wind controls the two other defects Bile and Phlegm, and mixes with them. Wind indicates the psychosomatic aspect in Tibetan medicine because it includes the mind, alone, or in conjunction with Bile or Phlegm.

There are five types of *Wind,* which control movement of pulse, breath, circulation, and connection to the consciousness of the body.

1. *The Life sustaining Wind,* which assists breath, has its seat in the crown of the head. From there it moves through the throat and chest down to the solar plexus. This is connected to

Hearing,

Feelings and thought,

Controls the swallowing of food,

Breathing,

Spitting,

Belching and

Sneezing.

When it functions properly, it actually clears all the five senses, and the intellect.

It stabilises and embraces the mind.

If you swallow without chewing properly, you certainly get a problem with the *Life sustaining Wind.* Make a little observation – when you eat out, study the people around you as they eat. It is easy to sort those who scarcely take time to chew, but gulp down their food. Guaranteed Wind! But if, at the same time, they chew so energetically that it looks as if they are in anger, Bile is included too!

Imbalance in the Life sustaining Wind appears as:

Worries,

Anxiety,

An overactive brain,

Insomnia,

Neurological disturbances,

Hiccups,

Headaches due to stress, and

Asthma – the latter combined with Phlegm.

2. *The ascending Wind,* which assists speech, has its seat in the chest. It is also connected with the tongue, the uvula, the throat and the nose. Thus connected with speech, it develops mental activity, strengthens the body and promotes a healthy skin.

It connects past, present and future and preserves memory, logic and sound judgement.

A person who squabbles, or at least speaks too fast – and too much, has his problem with one's speech, such as stammering or dysphasia, a dry cough, sore throat and exhaustion, surely has imbalance in the ascending Wind. Although it could also stem from shocks or displaced memories from childhood.

3. *The Pervasive Wind,* which assists all types of muscular movements and circulation, has its seat in the heart, but goes to all parts of the body, the inner organs, the skin and the senses.

It regulates the rhythm of the heart, and the expansion and contraction of the blood vessels.

It also distributes nourishment to the seven physical constituents, the essential: nutrients, blood, muscles, fat, bone structure, bone marrow and the regenerative substances.

A person having palpitations, and who is frantic in pressing situations, his nourishment passes too quickly through the body so that the seven physical constituents do not synthesise properly.

4. *The fire-like accompanying (metabolic) Wind,* which aids digestion and the assimilation of nourishment.

When the firelike Wind has its seat in the stomach, but goes to all parts of the digestive system – the stomach, the large and the small intestine, and passes through all the cavities of the body.

Here the essential nutrients are separated from the residual products, the rubbish. This Wind is the basis for all growth.

When the Fire-like Wind is in imbalance, digestion becomes too quick or too slow, there may be a nervous stomach, too much wind (air).

The assimilation of nourishment is poor, and so is the formation of new tissue.

5. *The Descending Wind,* which assists the excretion of urine and faeces, has its seat in the perennial area. It goes to the intestines, the bladder, the reproductive organs and the thighs.

It has the task of releasing or retaining sperm, menstruation, stools, urine and the foetus correctly.

Any problem with regard to releasing or retaining any of the excretions above is surely a problem of Descending Wind.

We in the West lead a hectic life, and do not take time to go to the toilet. Not just now! It must wait.

Pain in the lower part of the back is another imbalance, as well as stomach cramps and colitis.

* For details see Appendix III

Take one example of Wind problem:

> MR. HOWARD is a man in his 70's, who has suffered from chronic constipation for many years. Dr.Thokmay Paljor* found digestion was very weak and very cold, which in turn affected all the organs. Questioning the man's diet, it was found that he hungered for everything sweet. Not only for cakes, jams and desserts, but also for candies. Lots of candies, even when he woke up at night, which he usually did. Further, he added a bit proudly, that he only used sugar-free candies. The Tibetan doctor then explained to him that sweetness whether from sugar, artificial sweeteners or other sources, are all just as detrimental. He advised the patient most emphatically to drop what was sweet, as too much sweet creates Wind and cold. Besides, Sweet being the combination of the Earth and Water elements, both having cold and heavy characteristics, it harms the digestive heat. The patient had a healthy diet apart from all the sweets, but was advised to use warming food as well as cooked lamb, chicken, duck and soups with hot spices.

All food and drink have their Wind, Bile and Phlegm characteristics, in addition to being characterised as to whether they create heat or cold in the body. They are also connected to the seasons. The most difficult months for a Wind person (in the Northern hemisphere) are November through February because he suffers from wind and cold, and not least a dry cold.

Wind symptoms are generally worst in the evening and before dawn. "Dry" disorders, such as constipation, eczema and psoriasis are Wind-based. That also means that dry food is not good for him, such as biscuits and dried fruits. So do note that constipation, eczema and psoriasis are typical dry illnesses.

> Mr. Dean: I had suffered from eczema for the last three years. I consulted Dr. Tsewang Tamdin,* who gave me advice regarding diet, and to drink enough water. I received medical treatment for ten months, and was then completely cured. After two months the eczema had dried up. New

* For details see Appendix III

attacks were mild, and after another six months on Tibetan medicine, I was cured and the eczema never returned.

Asthma and most rheumatic ailments are a combination of Wind and Phlegm.

Further problems of Wind can arise from over-indulgence as well as completely abstaining from something. For example mental activity to the extreme, can lead to fanaticism.

Psychic conditions connected to Wind are:

Haste,

Loquacity,

Nervousness,

Anxiety,

Sleeplessness,

Pain,

Shivering and

Cramps.

Wind gets worse during sorrow, shock and melancholy.

The Wind type is skinny, with protruding joints and bone ends. His muscles are poorly developed. The skin is dry and bluish.

The main seats of Wind are:

large intestine,

heart,

bone structure,

ears and

skin.

Think movement of these five points. Wind moves thought and speech, breath, the pulse beat in the heart and the blood, assists the digestion, the intestines and defecation, moves the muscles through the central nervous system, and moves the expansion and contraction in the tissue.

Wind represents the air element, and is described as coarse, light, cold, subtle (can pass through narrow passages), hard and mobile, and needs its opposites if out of balance.

The opposite for coarse is oily food like butter, cheese and soups. A light person needs heavy food, which does not pass too quickly through the digestive system.

A cold peson requires warm food, warm clothes, warm friends and warm climate. Subtle and hard is balanced by oily food. Mobile is balanced by stable.

To counteract dryness, you need bread instead of dry biscuits, porridge instead of muesli. Soups and porridge are excellent.

If there is imbalance in one or more of these qualities - either being too much, too little or disturbed, this results in illness.

Signs of illness : As indicated above, the Wind disorder and their symptoms are primarily found

in the pelvis area,
in the joints,
the skin and the large intestine,
especially the ascending and the transverse colon,
and in the ears.

The large intestine is the most central area.

There are many outer signs of Wind imbalance – defects in the bone structure, such as a bent or curved spine, spine injuries, scoliosis, and wrong positions in the spinal and neck cord, pelvis, arms and legs.

Wind rules all biological movements, which further leads to changes in metabolism.

The Tibetan doctors who have been to Europe and America worry about the stress of the West. We run faster and faster to overcome more and more, and get sicker and sicker, they say. And the heartfelt sigh of Dr. Wangyal after his first visit – "you have so many Wind illnesses!"

The Wind type should definitely live a calmer life, without much noise, sleep regularly and eat regularly, and avoid stress, especially on an empty stomach.

Another very important advice – divide the stomach into four, where two parts should be filled with food, one part with liquid, and the fourth part should be left empty, as it is the latter part which gives room for mastication and synthesis of the food and drink. When you eat too little; or fill up the stomach all the time, or eat till your belly is completely full, you threaten your health!

Tibetan medicine stresses that one should not repress any of the natural urges of the body, such as hunger, thirst, yawning, sneezing, belching, the signals of sleep, flatulence, the need to urinate and defecate. But in our "civilised" world certain sounds are very impolite, and in our stressed world we do not have time to go to the toilet – we postpone it again and again. This however, can result in chronic problems like asthma, skin diseases, rheumatic problems – and cancer.

You would be able to recognize Wind in people around you. I have a couple of Danish friends, both of who are *Wind,* in temperament as well as in age.

> JONNA and Ib are lovely people, gay, hospitable, inspiring, very fond of dancing and singing. Still they face problems, because they react before thinking. They decided that their house was too big, and sold it before having found a new one. They rented for more than a year until they found a new house. Again it was too big a house! So they sold again, and have been renting ever since. Though they are still looking for a house to buy.

Another couple of my friends, as charming as Jonna and Ib, and also as indecisive.

> BRIT got cancer, was operated and no spreading was found. Still, the doctors decided on radiography and chemotherapy, to be on the safe side. I suggested her to consult a Tibetan doctor, but she is so disheartend that all initiative was suppressed, even though she keep contacting me for advice.

The Tibetan doctor – oh, yes !

But she never got there. She is now suffering badly from the after effects of the treatment. She is willing to "try everything", but never gets that far. Fortunately, not all Wind people are so uncertain!

Fire, depicted emitting from the dragon's jewel.

Bile (*Pitta* in Ayurvedic medicine) is the heat energy. The Tibetan word for Bile is "flames". (Which was typical of Mr. Bile!)

We find it especially in:

the blood

the sweat glands,

the liver,

the gall bladder

the small intestine, and

the eyes.

Its centre is in the middle part of the body.

Are you a Bile person?

The Bile person has a yellowish complexion and a strong metabolism. The skin is reddish, often freckled. His hair is red or reddish blond. He may turn bald, get receding hair growth or grey hair at an early age.

The Bile person is brave, likes challenges, has a sharp brain and can be very arrogant. He is often a workaholic, always on time, feels excessive hunger and thirst, though he may not eat much at meals. He does not like to wait long for the next meal, though, so he is impatient if the meal is late. And he loves rummaging in the refrigerator between meals. He may wake up at night, feeling hungry or thirsty. When thirsty, it is a sign that he needs to quench the fire. He likes sweet, sour, bitter and cooling food.

He sweats easily and emits a foul body odour. He prefers cool weather. He is happy in winter without scarf, cap or gloves and does not bother to button his jacket. Indoors he may complain that the room is overheated. So sun bathing is not for him, nor hot baths, nor strong sex.

To be in balance, he should be moderate in everything, avoid stress, enjoy nature, especially by the sea or in the mountains, enjoy relaxing hobbies, and meditate. Good colours are the cooling green and blue, but definitely not red, being a "hot" colour!

When strongly out of balance, the patient should be treated firmly, at times even very determined. The Tibetan doctor always shows his compassion. But here he may, as reluctant as he would be, find it necessary to use harsh words to get his message through.

There are also five types of Bile:

1. *Digestive Bile* has its seat between the stomach and the small intestine, that is between the digested and the undigested food. This is the most important and most complicated of the five Bile types, and regulates the metabolism.

Digestive Bile breaks down the essential nutrients from food and liquid, and then it separates the essential from the residual products. It promotes the digestive heat and bodily heat all over, and eases the function of the following four types of Bile. It also signalises whether you are hungry or thirsty. The Bile person chews energetically. So energetically, that at times it looks like he is angry, attacking the food on the plate as he chews.

When this type of Bile is out of balance, digestion can either be too fast or too slow, too weak or too efficient. This can give an acrid smell, heartburn (cardialgia), stomach ulcer or piles.

Do not ignore the signals of the body, or the signals of hunger or thirst, or of your first reactions to strong spices or alcohol.

> TIM was a most complacent chap. Of late he had become very fond of hot spices, and of beer. His blood pressure soared, and his doctor gave him pills, then more pills, for the side

effects. When told that his problems were due to being too hot, he would not believe it. His imbalance had made him stubborn.

2. *Accomplishing Bile* has its seat in the heart. It provides satisfaction, holds determination, stimulates a good memory and a clear intelligence, and maintains concentration. It is the seat for the original impulse of the mind for ambition and fulfilment, for pride and wishes.

When in balance, the Bile type has a warm heart and is genuinely obliging.

When out of balance the person makes wrong decisions or takes risks, while burning in the inferno of fury.

3. *Colour transforming Bile* has its seat in the liver and spleen.

It sustains and develops the formation of the red blood cells. It is responsible for the haemoglobin in the blood, muscle tissue and subsequent bodily constituents. Consequently it balances the chemistry of the blood.

When in balance, the person is glowing with satisfaction, is effective, and knows when to relax.

When out of balance he is critical, also of self, speaks straight from the liver. He is tyrannical, jealous, hot tempered, bears a grudge, is angry, hateful and aggressive. He swears, is rough handed, destroys things and may hurt or kill in a rage.

When out of balance he may suffer jaundice, colitis, anaemia, diverse blood and skin diseases.

Do you know someone who has had the bile bladder removed? I know three – all Bile persons! That does not prove that everyone who has the bile bladder removed, is a Bile person, but they are certainly in the lead.

4. *Visual Bile* has its seat in the eyes, which improves the sight, and also has the ability to make subtle judgement.

In balance the person has a warm expression. When out of balance, his eyes are red or yellow. When blinded by hate, he sees red.

5. *Complexion-clearing Bile* has its seat in the skin. When in balance, it shows a clear skin with a healthy complexion.

When out of balance, the feelings show in the skin flushing, red with anger. In stress rashes appears on the skin. The skin may become infected. The person sweats a lot, hands and feet are clammy; the smell of the sweat is acrid. Acne, herpes and skin cancer belongs to this Bile when it is out of balance.

Bile, which represents the Fire element, has the following characteristics –

Sharp: The stomach is acid and generally there is too much acidity. But sharp also means that the person has a sharp intellect!

Oily: The skin and hair are somewhat oily, as bile is very much associated with the gall bladder.

Hot: A warm body, and a warm heart. Being predominantly of blood, it is hot in nature.

Light: The underlying effect of mind has the light characteristic.

Pungent: Sour body smell, foul smell of breath, stinking smell of urine and faeces.

Purgative: Sweats easily, has clammy hands and feet, as mentioned above. Has frequent tendency to a loose motion.

To sum up, the Bile energy, which represents the Fire element, i.e., the heat, is everywhere in the body. It regulates the body temperature, digestion, the take-up and distribution, assimilation and metabolism.

It is also responsible for intelligence, clear thought and understanding. Provides a clear skin, and *shows* thirst and hunger.

Signs of illness: The main seats of Bile, with its symptoms and its illnesses, are primarily

in the blood,
the sweat glands,
the liver,
the gall bladder,
the small intestine,
the eyes,

and also shows in the skin
and in the serous fluid.

Liver and bile illnesses, rheumatic fever and fever illnesses, plus several eye ailments, are connected with Bile.

An aggressive psychical illness is a kind of schizophrenia. The patient is agitated; marked by excessive and often wild, motor activity and agitation.

Bile disorders arise when one craves for hot spices and food items with a warm potency (see p. 44), as for instance, lamb, mutton, duck, liberal portions of butter, sharp tasting food, much sugar, hot spices and alcohol.

> GARY – "I suffered from liver inflammation with fever. I had severe pains for two months, went to see an allopathic doctor, supported by various tests. After one month a friend recommended me to try Tibetan medicine, and in the short period of two weeks the disease had almost vanished."

> MR. SHORE – "I suffered from Amoebic hepatitis. For one and a half years before treatment, I had been subject to a number of ailments, mainly inability to stomach food and to retain it. Also boils sprang up all over my body and a constant sour taste of bile was in my mouth. After two months on Tibetan medicine I was cured of amoebic hepatitis. After another two months my boils had subsided and I was fully cured."

A pair of rhinoceros horns symbolises happiness.

Phlegm (*Kapha* in Ayurvedic medicine) is the cold energy, which is developed by delusion (confusion). Phlegm is the liquid energy, i.e., all the biological liquids, which are mainly formed by the elements of Water and Earth (see p. 33). Phlegm's main seat is in the cell membranes.

Unlike Greek medicine, Tibetan philosophy and medicine do not consider only the four elements – Earth, Water, Fire and Air only – but also add a fifth element, namely, Space.

Remember, the reason for not filling the fourth part of the stomach is that it needs space for the digestive process. When the stomach is too full, there is no space for digestion.

The Phlegm, and energy means all body fluids in Tibetan medicine:

Intestinal fluids,

lymph,

phlegm, and

mucus.

Because liquid is its main ingredient, Phlegm is responsible for the biological strength and the natural resistance in the tissue, produces digestive juices, lubricates the joints, gives a clear and smooth skin, supports the memory and stimulates sleep.

Perhaps you are a Phlegm type?

Phlegm represents the Earth and Water elements, so characteristics of a Phlegm person are:

Oily – He has oily hair and skin.

Cold – He may get depressed in cool, humid weather, usually worst by the end of the winter and the early spring, may have a slow digestion and a high cholesterol level.

Heavy – He is down to earth, sleeps heavily, loves comfort, likes to lounge on the sofa or in a reclining chair, is fond of food and fat (may eat too much for comfort). He is fond of sour, acrid, bitter and rough food, and when out of balance, eats too much fat, sugar, salt, fried food, heavy food, dairy products – especially cheese, milk and ice cream. Eats a lot, even if he is not hungry. And you can see by the way he is eating, that he really enjoys every mouthful.

Greedy – He is fond of money and material things. Also likes to "own" people, clings heavily to them and broods over them. On the other hand, the person who is in balance has an inner security and stability.

Soft – Being soft spoken and with a soft nature, he has the ability to attract people. A gliding gait, smooth skin, his manners and the expression in his eyes are soft.

Stable – Psychologically he is tolerant, quiet, generous, friendly, helpful and compliant. He is content with life, respects others' feelings, and is not easily influenced by change.

The phlegmatic person is blessed with much wealth, health, prosperity, sleep and long life. He tends to live longer than the Wind and Bile person. This is certainly noticeable in our stressful society, and it is because he does not stress easily. However, when he feels stressed, ambivalent, and unwanted – he withdraws.

There are also five types of Phlegm :

1. *Supporting Phlegm,* with its seat in the chest, supports the other four Phlegm-types.

It regulates the functions of all liquids in the body, and supports the Water and Earth elements.

When this type of Phlegm is out of balance, you get all types of lung problems, asthma, bronchitis, or a heart attack, etc. Smoking can worsen the condition.

> MRS. KATE: "I had suffered from asthma for the last thirty years. Then consulted Dr. Tenzin Choedrak*, and about a year and a half later I was totally cured. But continued to take the Tibetan medicine as a precautionary measure. Even strenuous work does not affect me now."

2. *Decomposing Phlegm,* with its seat in the upper part of the digestive system, where the food is not yet digested. It has a great responsibility. The three subtle heats of digestion always play an important role here. It is responsible for the synthesis of the seven physical constituents, (also see p. 28) which are:

the essential nutrients of food,

---

* For details see Appendix III

the blood,
the muscle tissue,
the fat,
the bone structure
and the regenerative fluids,
plus the three excretions – faeces, urine and sweat.

Its physical function is to masticate the solid food particles into finer particles and to mix it well with the liquid portion.

The reason why the mixing Phlegm is so important is really easy to understand. Phlegm gives humidity to the stomach walls. When this does not happen, the digestion gets too dry, heavy and slow.

We tend not to drink sufficiently with the meal. When this type of Phlegm is not liquid enough, the food particles are not dissolved, and they will remain in the tissue, poisoning the body. Indigestion and long term chronic ailments crop up here.

3. *Experiencing Phlegm,* with its seat in the tongue.

It senses and experiences the six primary tastes, namely, sweet, sour, salt, bitter, acrid and astringent.

If you eat too much or too often, the taste buds lose their ability. Give yourself time to register the six tastes – it might give you a signal that this is not what I should have. A good warning! Or, it tells you – I can never get enough of that! That certainly is the traitor – the false warning, the craving! The most usual craving is a sweet tooth.

The same thing happens when you exaggerate some tastes. That is, when you have a craving, be it food, drink or tobacco.

When the taste disappears, other Phlegm problems often appear, such as obesity, food allergies (cravings), clogging (i.e., sinusitis) and diabetes.

> MR. BARNES: "I have been suffering from sinusitis for 15-20 years, and tried a lot of allopathic medicines. After taking Tibetan medicine for 45 days I was cured! I have had no

problems since, and am relaxed."

DAVE L., a businessman, age 61: "In addition to diabetes, I suffered from skin problems and some black spots in the skin, troubling me since I was 22. I also had a boil on my back, oozing matter. The boil proved difficult to cure, and was dangerous. After consulting Dr Dorjee Rapten Neshar*, the boil disappeared completely and the level of blood sugar became normal. The black spots in the skin are also disappearing. The treatment with Tibetan medicines was far more effective than the English medicines. Took longer, but with total cure. No side effects."

4. *Satisfying Phlegm* has its seat primarily in the head, but functions from the neck upwards.

It increases and satisfies the strength of the five senses. Which means that it maintains the humidity in the nose, the mouth, the eyes, the sinuses and the spinal fluid.

When out of balance this type of fluid either floods or gets congested, and may result in sinusitis, hey fever, loss of smell and generally weakened senses.

5. *Connecting Phlegm*, with its seat in all the joints, lubricates them, so that the limbs can stretch and contract. And what lubricates? Enough liquid, chewing properly, and leaving space in the stomach for digesting.

Too much Wind dries out the joints, with arthritis as a result. Too much Bile gives infection in the joints, i.e. rheumatism, and too much Phlegm gives joints that are unstable, filled with yellowish liquid. However, most Phlegm diseases start in the chest and spread to the head.

Signs of Illness: Phlegm disorders arise primarily with symptoms

in the chest,
throat,
stomach,
kidneys,
spleen,
bladder,
lungs,

* For details see Appendix III

and the head.

In addition, Phlegm disorders reside in the muscles, the fat, the marrow, the regenerative substances, in the urine and faeces, in the stomach where the food is digested, and in the tongue and nose, kidneys, spleen, bladder and lungs.

The phlegmatic person has a poor digestive heat, as Phlegm is by nature cold. He should therefore avoid too much fat, sweet, bitter, heavy and cool food (like raw vegetables and ice cream), and too many cool drinks. And definitely shun fast foods.

> ANDRINE: "I am a fat person and used to feel waterlogged and heavy. I also suffered from stomach-ache, heartburn and wind, even if I ate light non-fat food. I felt lazy and lethargic. After a week on Tibetan medicines, I felt that half of my problems had gone, and after another few weeks I was nearly back to my normal self."

The Phlegm person should not be subjected to cold and damp places. They make him depressed. If he exercises enough, that would be very good, as it creates heat and subdues depression.

When out of balance he needs to be stimulated and inspired, and to vary the contents of the day. He hesitates long in making a decision, becomes easily passive in all ways. He may become too strongly attached to others. When his craze for owning things gets out of balance he becomes mean, craves apportions in stead of shares. He becomes overprotective. He postpones decisions, sleeps too much, and become lethargic.

He may become forgetful, have fits of vertigo, and the eyes have a tendency to roll upwards. Physically he reacts when it is too humid, clammy and cold, the nose runs, or saliva from the mouth, the sinuses are blocked. He may suffer from oedemas, congested chest, is pale. The joints could be swollen, unstable or aching, the limbs feel heavy. He catches colds easily, puts on weight, cholesterol becomes high, there may be allergies or asthma.

Phlegm is also phlegm literally, and asthma is to a great extent a Phlegm illness, or rather a Phlegm + Wind illness. Similar typical Phlegm diseases are influenza, sinus problems and types of arthritis. Diabetes is also a Phlegm illness.

Phlegm excesses are due to abundant food and drink, so here self-control is important. As Phlegm is cold, foods that help, without excesses, have a warm, light, sharp and mobile character.

Wind disorders, then, can be of both cold and hot nature, while Bile disorders are always hot, and Phlegm disorders always cold.

However, most people do not have a one-defect disease, but a combination.

Wind + Phlegm is cold,

Wind + Bile is warm,

Bile + Phlegm are cold and hot in combination,

the same being the case with Wind + Bile + Phlegm.

In addition you have blood combinations, blood having a warm character.

Confusing? Yes. But you can try out food and listen to the body, which often gives you the answers.

Have you found out who you are? The following story may confirm your diagnosis:

> There were three friends, each with a different nature: One a Wind dominant, the other Bile dominant and the third Phlegm dominant. It was cold and none of them were really warmly dressed. On one particular evening they agreed to go to a restaurant to eat and relax after a stressful day's work. They entered a crowded, noisy room that was not warm enough. They ordered some cold, soft drinks and started chatting. After a while they asked for some rice, vegetables, pork and a salad. All of them ate a lot, and after that they drank strong coffee. As it got late, it was time for the restaurant to close. They came out of the restaurant and it was quite windy and cold. After about a mile's walk in the cold and windy night they reached home. There they continued to chat till dawn, stimulated by more coffee.

> It is cold and windy outside, noisy and crowded inside, none of them were dressed warmly enough, the food they had eaten was mainly unwholesome, because it was cold and light in quality – same as the surroundings and their not warm enough clothes. The drinks were totally cool and light, they were engaged in excessive talking, and they barred themselves from sleep.

This is the story of three friends at a particular time. Although they are different in nature, they have experienced the same food and drink, the same behaviour and the same climate on that particular occasion. What then happened to each of them regarding the state of their energies, of their particular health?

Under these conditions the Wind dominant person was most affected, followed by the Phlegm dominant person, while the Bile dominant person was least affected. In other words, the Wind dominant person will have a serious Wind disorder, the Phlegm dominant person a moderate Wind disorder, and the Bile dominant person will only have a slight Wind disorder.

This is because the quality and the characteristics of the diet, behaviour and the climatic conditions of that particular eventing, corresponds much more to the characteristics of the Wind energy, less in the case of the Phlegm energy and very much less in the case of the Bile energy.

That means that the Wind person is more susceptible to the Wind arising conditions, the Phlegm person less and the Bile person very little. This clearly shows how important a role the person's nature or temperament plays in one's state of health. It is not the temperament in itself that gets imbalanced, but the principle energies of the mind and body brings about the disorder.

The characteristics of the types of the Wind, Phlegm and Bile persons are inherent. They are the natural features that a person acquires while in the mother's womb and are then born with. And this remains unchanged throughout the person's lifetime.

As mentioned above, it is not at all clear-cut whether one is purely of a Wind, Bile or Phlegm nature. There are seven person types:

Wind
Bile
Phlegm
Wind + Bile
Wind + Phlegm
Bile + Phlegm, and
Wind + Bile + Phlegm.

The combinations of the four latter types usually result in persons who are more balanced in character and lifestyle. It is difficult to draw divisions, though, as everyone seems to have a little of each person type in them. Sound judgement and long experience is necessary to judge the person – and you may be your best judge.

It is not only the three defects with their variables that must be brought into balance. So must the proportions of hot and cold in the body, the main excretions: Urine, faeces and sweat, and the seven physical constituents.

The flute symbolizes the gentleman's need to master music.

The Seven Physical Constituents

When the three energies Wind, Bile and Phlegm are in balance, they can help our body to develop the seven physical constituents. The food we eat is dissolved by Phlegm, which is the liquid energy, warmed by Bile, which is the heat energy, and separated by Wind – the moving energy.

The seven physical constituents are formed by what the body picks up from the food we eat.

They are

The essential nutrients of the food,
Blood,
Flesh and muscles,
Fat,
Bones,
Bone marrow,
and the three excretions.

Excretions, what is not of any use to nourishment of the body is excreted as urine, faeces and sweat. In other words, if the three energies are in balance, the body makes use of all the essential nourishment, and excretes in full what is not needed. That is perfect health.

When one or more of the three energies are imbalanced it is contrary to perfect health. Then there will also be imbalances in the essential nutrients, and in the excretions. You may suffer diarrhoea, constipation, problems with urination, and too much or too little sweat. It is like a factory – when there is a strike, the production stops. A quality product depends equally on the raw material, the machines and the workers. If one of the elements is below par, the end product is not good.

We can compare the balancing of the three energies Wind, Bile and Phlegm, the seven elements and the three excretions, with seed and fruit.

When you sow a seed of chilli, you get chilli. When you eat the chilli, which is warm, you develop heat in the digestive process. If you eat too much food that is warm, or has a warm character, such as strong spices, the digestive process will be too warm.

When you plant a potato, you get potatoes. When you eat a potato, which is cold, you develop coldness. If you eat too much food that is cold, or has a cold character, the digestive system becomes too cold. When you develop too much cold or heat in the body, you get out of balance.

Are you by nature cold? (a Phlegm or Wind character), you will need warming food.

Are you by nature warm? (a Bile character), you need food that is cooling.

If you start to sweat when you eat strongly spiced food, the sweat tries to cool down (water quenches the fire). From time to time it can manage to quench, but not again and again!

If you shiver eating ice cream or banana, the shivering is a desperate attempt by the body to create heat. Again, it works from time to time, but not repeatedly.

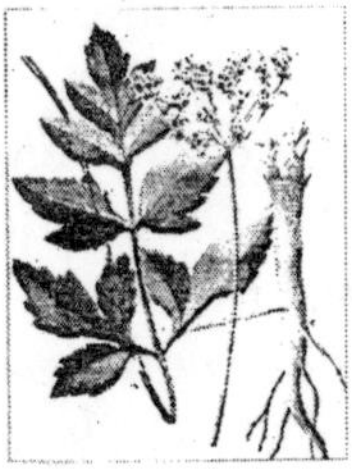

*Heracleum candicans WALL**

Only the root is used for wind disorders and inflammation caused by vulnerable fever.

---

* A drawing by Dr. Dawa, from his book *A Clear Mirror of Tibetan Medicinal Plants.*

The unending knot symbolises love and devotion

If the basic human nature had been aggressive,
we would have been born with animals'
claws and beast of preys' teeth,
while ours are very short, very pretty and very weak!
And that signifies that we are not equipped to be
aggressive beings.
Even the size of our mouth is limited.
Therefore my opinion is that the basic nature of
man is friendly.

H.H. the Dalai Lama

The conch shell calls to prayer

Chapter - II

DIGESTION

The Tibetan doctors observe the six sense organs representing sight, hearing, smell, taste, touch and thought. In Tibetan medicine the most important organ is the brain, the sixth sense organ which regulates all the information to the conscience! We westerners do not include the brain as a sense organ. Why on earth not. It is definitely a very important and ruling sense organ!

The six vessel organs are – the stomach, large and small intestines, gall bladder, urinary bladder, and the testis or ovaries.

The five vital organs are – the heart, liver, lungs, spleen and kidneys.

To understand the principles of diet according to Tibetan medicine, it is necessary to go into its theories.

It is fascinating too, as it goes much further than Tibetan medicine and is the key to Tibetan philosophy. *And* to the understanding of nature!

All living, and non-living, is based on the same basic material of five elements.

The Five Elements:

1. Earth
2. Water
3. Fire

4. Air
5. Space

These five elements are present everywhere. In the forming of the whole universe, as well as our bodies, food and medicines. Our bodies are part of nature, and without the five elements no life can exist, nor any conscience. The three energy-processes Wind, Bile and Phlegm are influenced by these five elements, and concern both body and mind.

According to Buddhist thinking, the universe, and everything in it, comes from spirit. We could perhaps compare it with – "In the beginning was the word" from the Christian Bible.

This spirit energy evolved into Space energy, which exists everywhere, and is at the same time an expression for the more *subtle* Air, Fire, Water, and Earth energies.

As Air (Wind) developed through a tremendous speed, it created heat: *The coarser Fire* was formed.

And as it dispersed, by the help of Air (Wind), an intense heat evolved, and this violent, abrupt energy formed *Water.*

As Water developed and increased, increased Wind combined with increased Fire created waves that created tiny particles of mass, and this is how *Earth* was formed.

In the Tibetan Buddhist cosmology, these five cosmic energies have an inherent force, or movement, that form physical qualities like

Solidity (mass) = Earth,
Floating condition = Water,
Hot and dynamic energy = Fire,
Growth and movement = Air, and
Development and expansion = Space.

These five basic elements are all present in every substance. Water is a classic example:

Water in its solid form, when it is frozen ice, is a manifestation of the Earth principle.

It is melted by heat = Fire,
So it changes into liquid = Water.
The Water evaporates expressing the Air-principle.
The vapour disappears into Space.

Another example: A carrot – the root is Earth, the carrot juice is Water, the protein energy is Fire, the growth is stimulated by Air (wind, movement), and Fire (the sun) and Water (the rain) and Space (expansion). Dr. Lobsang Wangyal commented that frozen vegetables and fruit lose their Fire in the deep freeze, which results in the loss of the protein energy.

The five elements are a complex atomic unit, and are classified according to the atomic units that dominate. The element Earth dominates when the atomic units have an overweight of earth, etc.

We say that the element Earth forms the base (mass), Water is binding, Fire is ripening, Wind stimulates growth and movement, and Space creates room for all development. Read that sentence again, thinking of an apple! Not so difficult to understand, after all!

Going back to Wind, Bile and Phlegm, we experience them at their basic level. Everything that belongs to the world we understand belongs to this level, where the energies have become compact.

These are the visible energies:

Earth and stone, where we sow and build,
Water, we drink and swim in,
Fire, we light and burn,
The air, we breathe and the wind that blows,
The space, we have around us and fly through.

What you and I are is based on the five elements on this basic, material level. So are the food we eat and the herbs/minerals in the Tibetan medicines – and all herbs and minerals of course. All have the five elements in them, but in different proportions.

Organic salts, water, organic carbohydrates and fats belong to the Water and Earth elements. The proteins are equivalent to the Fire element. The Air and Space elements help the other elements in their growth and development of nutrients.

In Tibetan medicine anatomy, physiology and pharmacology are based on the theory of the five elements. Through this arises the law of like and unlike, when regarding taste, how potent any type of food is, what disorders that must be balanced through diet, lifestyle, medicines and other therapies. Diet, lifestyle, medicines and therapies all take their starting-point from the five elements.

For instance, a weak digestion indicates that there is too little Fire, i.e., Digestive heat, and all food, medicines and therapies must contain the Fire element. A cold disease needs a warm treatment.

All living beings are extremely complex, because they consist of many systems. The higher developed the being, the more complex. This includes systems like digestion, excretions, respiration, circulation, propagation, the nervous system and the endocrine system – and it is impossible to separate them. They are all mutually dependent, inside the body as well as in relation to the environment. This means that all living beings reflect the macrocosm and are part of the cosmic picture.

As part of the living systems, man is a microcosm of nature. Therefore the five elements that are present in all matter are also present in every human being.

1. The body's solid parts such as bone, cartilage, nails, muscles, tendons, and nose, with its smell, come from the Earth element.
2. The excretion of digestive fluids, of phlegm, as well as blood, tongue with its taste and lymph belong to the Water element.
3. The body temperature, eyesight, digestion, assimilation and metabolism belong to the Fire element.

4. Space in movement = Air (Wind): Respiration, skin, the tactility, the heartbeats, the movement of the muscles, expansion and contraction in the organs and all other movements, function through the Wind principle.
5. The cavities of the body, as ears with their sound, stomach, intestines, breathing organs, blood veins, lymph vessels, etc., all belong to the Space element.

The middle level is not so visible, but it can be felt and measured, as for instance gravity and electromagnetism. The way the five elements work, can explain the macrocosmic universe as well as the atoms' microcosm.

The gold coin: symbol of wealth.

Digestive Heat

Our healthy condition is dependent on digestive heat. In Tibetan medicine this can be explained in two ways:

a) The characteristics of the digestive heat, and

b) The digestive process.

a) The characteristics of digestive heat:

The digestive heat has a great responsibility. It is the proper functioning of the fire-like or accompanying Wind, decomposing Phlegm, and digestive Bile, which results in the physical constituents.

Let's repeat that, from the chapter on *Balance of temperaments* :

The fire-like (metabolic Wind) assists digestion and this is how the nourishing part of the food is assimilated. Its seat is in the stomach, but goes to all parts of the digestive system –

the stomach, the small and large intestines. Together with the digestive Bile it separates the essential part of the food you have eaten, from the residual. This Wind is the basis for all growth, and it controls the food, via the stomach and the small intestine, from passing too quickly to the large intestine. Which may happen when you eat too fast, or are over- stressed.

Decomposing or mixing Phlegm, has its seat in the upper part of the digestive system, where the food is not yet digested. Here the solid food particles are broken down to finer particles and mixed with the liquid portion. The liquid you then get, gives humidity to the stomach walls. When it is digested, it passes the job on to the small intestine and digestive Bile.

As Phlegm concerns liquid, it is important that you drink enough. And nothing is healthier than water. It may even be better to drink warm boiled water than iced water. Freshly boiled water is smooth as velvet to the stomach, while iced water may be a shock – unless your digestion is too hot. You may add some fresh lemon or orange, for taste. If you drink fresh water from the tap, leave the water for half an hour or an hour in an open jar, this will cause some of the added chemicals to evaporate.

Digestive Bile is hot by nature, and has its seat below the stomach and above the intestines – it plays a vital role in the digestive process. Here the gradual splitting up begins. Digestive Bile resides between the stomach and the large intestine, between the undigested food, and the food that is already digested. Its task is to digest and separate the refined from the unrefined food.

After the nourishment has passed on to the liver, there are also excretions from the liver to the gall bladder, from the muscles to the fat cells, and from the fat to sweat. From the bone marrow the residue helps to moisten the intestines.

Digestive heat is then responsible for the excretions – faeces, urine and sweat, as well as for skin pigmentation, life span and bodily strength.

The essential nutrients, consists of

1. The vital essential part of what has been eaten,
2. The blood, which establishes life energy
3. And this in turn stimulates the growth of muscles,
4. The body fat, which lubricates the body,
5. The bone substance, i.e., structure and density,
6. The bone marrow, which includes the brain, the central nervous system
7. And the regenerative fluids.

Each one of the constituents is transformed by the assistance of the former, a proper chain reaction!

The final product of the total digestive process passes to what the Tibetans call, the *mDang*, that is the ultimate vital essence of our body.

Any changes in the digestive heat results in digestive problems, such as diarrhoea, constipation, bloating of the stomach.

When digestion is too fast, too much acid is produced, which can cause problems such as stomach ulcers. A stressed rhythm, whether eating or working, and an unbalanced psychic condition, are hard tasks for the digestion.

Correct digestive heat is the core to good health. This is built up through good habits. Eating warm and properly cooked food, food that is not too heavy to digest, choosing food with light and hot potency, (greasy food is heavy and hot, a raw salad is heavy and cold), keeping the body warm and by regular exercise. In addition one must adjust to the seasons, with cooling food in the heat of the summer, warming food in the cold of winter. Just as important is a healthy lifestyle and behaviour.

Some Tibetan medicines, like Pomegranate 4, may be recommended during the coldest part of winter, as it reactivates the digestive heat, gives a healthy skin, propels regular emptying of faeces from the intestine and urine from the bladder, stimulates the appetite and increases life span.

b) The digestive process:

When the food has been chewed and broken down into smaller particles, *Life supporting Wind* helps to push the food through the gullet (oesophagus) down to the stomach.

As mentioned before, the stomach is divided into four equal parts. We should not fill up more than three parts. The fourth part then gives the necessary space to digest the food. If the mixing Phlegm, the breaking down Bile and the fire like Wind do not get enough space (the element Space) then the digestion will not function properly.

If the nature of your food is light, you can eat a little more, as it is easier to digest. If you are eating some food of a heavy nature, you should always regulate the amount before you get to the feeling that you have eaten enough, since heavy food needs more time to digest: The less you eat of the heavy food, the less pressure there will be on your digestive system.

The three fruits: The peach is a symbol of immortality, the pomegranate is a symbol of fertility, the inedible, fragrant citron (lemon) symbolizes Buddha's grasping hand and stands for happiness.

Yes and No Food

Now to the easier part – with practical advice instead of theories, which are alien to Western thought. The list below is the ideal list, but do not be a slave to it. Listen to your body! Few of us have pure Wind, Bile or Phlegm imbalances. Usually there is a mixture, though one is more or less markedly in the lead.

a) Food for Wind Ailments:

As Wind is light and cold, we need warm food with a somewhat heavy (Earth) structure, which does not pass too quickly through the digestive system.

If you are nervous, porridge oats or a creamed vegetable soup is better than chocolate! Sugar makes you restless. It feels soothing at the moment of eating sugary things, but the after effect is negative. So people trying again for a soothing feeling, end up with increased restlessness. Artificial sweeteners are no better !

The No lists below are not absolute lists. These food items should be used sparingly though. And you may find that your body reports back that the No-food you are trying is really a No-food. If so, skip it for at least one month before another cautious try. It is greatly recommended not to use it daily, let at least four days pass each time.

Why not skip chocolates, candies, cookies, ice cream and whatever is sweet, for a month. Then choose one of the items and listen to the body's reactions. You may get a surprising answer! And with such an answer you will know how to avoid sweet things. After some months you may enjoy a sweet food from time to time, but not on a regular basis.

This skipping technique can be used for all food items, whether you suspect a Wind, Bile or Phlegm imbalance. A unique test of intolerance to food items! Choose accordingly!

Meat and fish:

Yes	**No**
Oily fish,	Pork,
lamb,	only a little beef.
duck,	
chicken,	
turkey and	
rabbit.	

The meat should be cooked slowly in a pot. Stews and soups are excellent Wind food. This is well-cooked, soft food that is easy to digest. Avoid fried food, baked is better.

Dairy products:

Yes	**No**
Hot milk,	Ice
cream	
butter.	

Grains:

Yes	**No**
Warm meals	Raw oats
wheat,	rice,
oats and	rye,
barley,	corn,
millet,	muesli.
porridge,	
buckwheat,	
freshly baked bread,	
fruit pies.	

Beans:

Yes	**No**
Chickpeas,	Other dried beans.
red lentils,	
mung beans.	

Herbs, spices and teas:

Yes	**No**
Basil,	Coriander,
oregano,	fenugreek,
aniseed,	parsley,
caraway,	saffron,
cumin,	turmeric.
clove,	ginger,
cinnamon,	cardamom,
liquorice root,	fennel,
nutmeg,	sage,
thyme,	mustard seeds.

The Ayurvedic Vata or Tibetan Wind tea.

Nuts: Use nuts if you want salty snacks. Nuts and almonds should be soaked, and perhaps ground, as tahini. This is oily food, which should not be used too much.

Fruits:

Yes	**No**
Pomegranates,	Unripe fruits
mangoes,	bananas
apples,	and citrus fruits,
pears,	red currants,
avocados,	cowberries.
apricots,	
bananas,	
raspberries,	
blackcurrants,	
fresh figs and dates,	
peach and	
pineapple.	

All in moderate portions, and dried fruit in very moderate portions. Generally add milk to sweet desserts. Stewed fruit is recommendable.

Vegetables:

Yes	**No**
Asparagus,	Raw salads,
beetroot,	broccoli,
carrot,	cabbage,
cucumber,	cauliflower,
green beans,	brussels sprouts,
onion and	celery,
garlic – but not raw,	aubergine,
long white radish.	green leafy vegetables,
	summer squash,
	tomatoes,

peppers,
peas,
potatoes,
mushrooms.

Always use oily dressings on salads, which should be at room temperature. Do not use many salads. You may use cabbages, though, add herbs to prevent air in the intestines, such as caraway, cumin, fennel or aniseed.

Fats: Sesame oil is very beneficial for Wind. Unrefined sugar and molasses is good for the mind.

Drinks: Freshly boiled water is excellent, and you may add a slice of fresh lemon or orange, however fruit juices are too sweet.

b) Food for Bile Ailments:

As Bile is warm, cool food is good – raw salads, pork, and cold drinks. As Bile is oily, one should avoid fatty food, whole milk, full-fat cheeses, fatty meat, fatty oils and fatty fish. Wheat should not be used much, as it is too heavy. Bile is sour, stinking, so avoid additives, coffee, tea and especially alcohol, which is very hot, as are hot and warm spices. Also avoid acidic food, vinegar, fermented food, and sour or fatty salad dressings. Soups are too hot. Strong spices and pickles likewise. Fast food and processed food are too salty and too sour. Bitter taste is very good, such as tonic water, and bitter greens like endive. Cool or fairly hot food is good, but not too hot. The structure should be moderately heavy.

Meat and fish:

Yes	**No**
Shrimps, lean fish, a little lean pork, chicken and turkey, egg whites.	Red meat, fat, smoked or tinned fish.

Dairy products:

Yes	**No**
Ice cream,	Yoghurt,
skimmed milk,	sour milk,
low-fat cheese,	full-fat cheese,
clarified butter,	cream,
light margarine.	sour cream,
	egg yolks.

Grains:

Yes	**No**
Rye,	Brown rice,
oats,	maize,
a little wheat,	millet,
rice,	rye,
muesli,	toast.
use many grains.	

Beans:

Yes	**No**
Chickpeas,	Lentils.
mung beans,	
tofu and	
other soy products.	

Herbs, spices and teas:

Yes	**No**
Liquorice root,	Pepper,
mint,	paprika sparingly,
dill,	cinnamon,
fennel,	cardamom,
saffron and	coriander,
turmeric.	salt,
	brown sugar.

Seeds :

Yes	No
Pumpkin seeds,	
sunflower seeds.	

Fruits:

Yes	No
Avocado,	Acidic fruits,
apples,	apricots,
cherries,	bananas,
grapes,	berries, especially
mango,	cowberries,
melon,	grapefruit,
pear,	peach,
raisin,	unripe fruits.
prune,	
(pineapple, plum),	
sugar cane.	

Vegetables:

Yes	No
Asparagus,	Beetroot,
broccoli,	aubergine,
brussels sprouts,	carrots,
cauliflower,	spinach,
celery,	tomatoes,
cucumber,	onions,
leafy vegetables,	garlic,
peppers,	radish.
summer squash,	
sprouts,	
potatoes,	
sweet potatoes.	

Fats:

Yes	No
Olive oil,	Almond oil,
Coconut oil,	corn oil,

Soy oil,	safflower oil,
Sunflower oil.	sesame oil.

Drinks:

Yes	**No**
Tonic water, and	Sour juices,
before the meal, mint tea	artificial stimulants,
	alcohol,
	coffee,
	tea,
	carbonated drinks,
	tobacco.

Alcohol with salt snacks is especially detrimental. So are artificial additives. Do not use too much food, too much salt, sour and spiced food nor too warm food especially during the summer. No pickles, ketchup, mustard, acid salad dressings, strong spices, honey or molasses.

c) Food for Phlegm Ailments:

As Phlegm is cold, you need warm food and drink. But it must not be too heavy in character. Lamb and duck are heavy, so chicken and turkey suits Phlegm better.

Wheat is heavy, so toasted bread is preferred. Porridge is heavy and too humid, and soups are for the cold season.

Be very careful with everything that has a concentrated sweet content ! Choose food with a lot of fibre, "smooth" food is also No-food. No deep fried food!

No cold salads, cold food straight from the refrigerator, and no deeply frozen vegetables. Fast food is too oily, salty and sweet.

Meat and fish:

Yes	**No**
Lean fish,	Oily fish,
no other seafood than shrimps,	pork,
chicken and	bacon,
turkey.	fatty meat like lamb and duck,

	sausages,
	deep fried food.

Dairy products:

Yes	**No**
Skimmed milk.	Whole milk,
	full-fat cheeses,
	butter.

Grains:

Yes	**No**
Buckwheat,	Wheat,
corn flour,	wheat bread
rye,	(unless toasted),
millet,	cakes,
only a little oats and rice.	muesli.

Beans:

Yes	**No**
Kidney beans	
tofu,	
soya beans.	

Herbs, spices and teas:

Yes	**No**
Fresh ground ginger,	
fenugreek,	
turmeric.	

Seeds:

Yes	**No**
Sunflower,	Almonds,
sesame.	nuts.

Fruits:

Yes	**No**
Apple,	Grapes,
apricot,	mango,

pear,	papaya,
pomegranate,	pineapple,
cowberries,	melon,
sparingly, dried fruit.	orange,
	plums.

Vegetables:

Yes	**No**
Asparagus,	Cucumber,
endive,	sweet potatoes,
beetroot,	pepper,
broccoli,	potatoes.
brussels-sprouts,	
cabbage,	
cauliflower,	
aubergine,	
garlic,	
onions,	
salad,	
leafy vegetables,	
peas,	
radish,	
spinach,	
sprouts,	
and mushrooms.	

Oils:

Yes	**No**
Corn,	Olive.
safflower,	
sesame,	
almond,	
sunflower.	

Drinks: Freshly boiled water, perhaps with a little fresh ginger in it.

Others: No sugar – try a little honey instead, but honey should not be cooked. Note that honey-bees are often fed on sugar. Genuine honey does not contain sugar, and behaves differently in the digestive process. Use desserts sparingly.

Don't take this as conclusive.

Listen to what your taste buds and your body tell you, and be honest about cravings!

As explained earlier in this article, if you suspect that you are intolerant to any food item, you may try it later after a month or so again.

Usually an illness is a combination of defects:

Wind + Bile: Wind inflates the heat of the Bile.

Wind + Phlegm: Increases cold, as they are both cold. But Wind also stimulates the Phlegm energy. Do not use too light or too heavy food.

The Lotus is one of the most precious Tibetan symbols - symbol of purity and perfection.

Hot and Cold Food

Grains are cold. Warm milk, butter or warming spices like cinnamon can balance porridge oats. Bread is cold, but is balanced by milk and butter. Dinner (rice, noodles, etc.) is cold, but is also balanced by butter, cheese and spices, plus the other food items for dinner. Fish and lamb/mutton is warming, game and beef is cool, pork is cold.

Warm items are onions, radish, cabbage, carrots and apple, herbs like aniseed, basil, peppermint and dill, eggs, peanuts and walnuts, aduki beans.

Garlic is cold as well as warm. Other cold items are cucumber, salad, spinach, pomegranate, cabbage, carrots and apples, sugar and honey.

A rule of thumb – most plants that grow under the earth are cold due to the predominance of Earth and Water elements.

Some Hints of Hot and Cold Food

Grains are cold. Warm milk, butter or warming spices like cinnamon can balance porridge oats. Bread is cold, but is balanced by milk and butter. Dinner (rice, noodles etc.) is cold, but is also balanced by butter, cheese and spices. Plus the other food items for dinner. Fish and lamb/mutton is warming, game and beef is cool, pork is cold. Warming items are onions, long radish, radish, cabbage, carrots and apple, herbs like aniseed, basil, peppermint and dill, eggs, peanuts and walnuts, aduki beans. Garlic is cold as well as warm. Cold items are cucumber, salad, spinach, pomegranate, cabbage, carrots and apples, sugar and honey. A rule of thumb: Most plants that grow under the earth are cold due to the predominance of Earth and Water elements.

A stylised flower in Tibetan carpets

Change of Diet

Change is part of life, but our ability to adjust to new environments also involves diet. The diet should support our health, our activities, our work and our mental aspiration. Our choice of food has a long-term effect on the body, and if we are not conscious of our choices, wrong diet will build up into chronic diseases. When in balance, our body conscience will lead us to choose the right food and the right amount. But our choices are more conscious and sure when we know our type and can analyse the food in accordance with it.

It is especially important to change the diet when ill, or in changed living conditions. If we choose correctly, we will soon notice improvement. However, it is not wise to change the diet abruptly. But it is necessary when there are acute problems, like dysentery.

Usually, a gradual change is recommendable. Drastic change of diet gives great fluctuations, and this means that the three temperaments are disturbed.

To understand the pattern of diet and proper lifestyle for individual illnesses, it is necessary to know the causes and other factors that influence the illness. By understanding the nature and cause of the illness, and how it is related to diet, is how one can help to heal oneself, or prevent getting ill. Sometimes it is easy, but more often not, so advice from a Tibetan doctor will be the sure way. To make it easier for you, when it is not so easy to find a Tibetan doctor near to where you live, an Ayurvedic doctor, and to some extent an acupuncturist, can also be of substantial help.

Chronic illnesses that are not genetic are usually caused by wrong diet and/or lifestyle. Wrong diet and lifestyle can also increase the problems where genetic disease is affected.

Right diet and lifestyle is also necessary as basis for prescribing the medicines. If you get medicines without changing the diet, the medicines will not be able to do their job. That is because you continue to do the wrong things for your health – an "anti-medicine". Your cravings are really strong "anti-medicine"!

Refined food, industrial food with artificial additives, artificial fertilizers, residues from pesticides, medicinal residues in fish and meat, several gene manipulated seeds and wrong treatment of raw foods will lead to internal toxins/ contamination. As also will too much fried food – it is better to bake it.

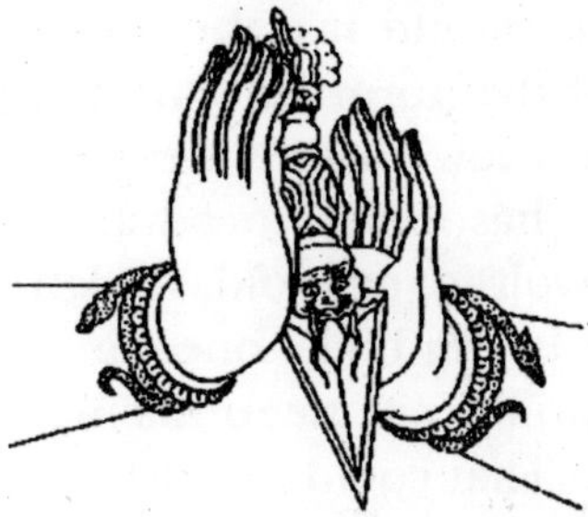

The dagger - a symbol equivalent to a sceptre.

Healthy Lifestyle and Actions

Always remember the true causes of illness: Wrong diet and wrong lifestyle. Which means misuse, overuse, under use of any food item and drink. Unhealthy lifestyle is: Wrong actions conducted through our body, our speech and our mind. This leads to imbalance and illness. Some examples:

When you talk and talk and talk – is overuse. Long term silence – is under use. Lies or ever using harsh words and swearing – is misuse. For proper digestion lifestyle is just as important as diet. There are three types of rules of life for good health: A. Daily lifestyle B. Seasonal lifestyle C. Impulses

A. *Daily lifestyle* is also divided into three:

1. Daily actions
2. Secular actions
3. Holy actions

1. Daily Actions:

Always be conscious that not only wrong diet, but also wrong lifestyle lead to illness.

Avoid negative actions for the body as well as for speech and mind. Do not expose yourself to what is not decent, and do not overstimulate the senses with impressions and sensual pleasures. Never be reckless or careless. Do not expose yourself to dangers.

As sleeping during the night has an irregular influence on the body, a relaxed position is important. If you miss a night's sleep, you should fast the following morning and then sleep half of the normal night during the daytime.

If energy is very low, or one is exhausted due to sorrow or over exertion, has experienced an extensive schedule with much talk involved, or is old, ridden by anxiety, or has too much poison in the body, one can eat fat, heavy food. Otherwise one should not sleep during the daytime, as it increases Phlegm. That could for instance induce swellings, cause headaches and drowsiness.

If one generally sleeps too much, one should take an enema, fast or enjoy the company of a woman! Avoid copulation with a pregnant woman, with one who is physically weak, ill or menstruates. The latter can induce illness in both man and woman because of the impure blood.

Warm milk or natural yoghurt will help against insomnia, and some alcohol – but only from time to time, do not make it a habit!

Regular massage with oil is good against ageing, tiredness and Wind problems. Periodic massage with oil on the crown of the head and on the feet makes the body light, increases vitality and increases the digestive heat. (Aromatherapy could also be a choice here). It could even induce loss of fat!

One should rub the body with (sesame) oil, followed by an application of ground lentil powder or barley flour, and then dry it off. That sounds a bit odd to us, but it is important, as it removes Phlegm.

Regular baths or showers increase energy, body heat, physical strength, life span and skin pigmentation, and removes itching caused by sweat, sleepiness, thirst and too much body heat. However washing the hair regularly in too hot water results in hair loss and impairs the sight.

Those with fever, with dysentery, with extended abdomen, having a cold, having digestive problems or problems with nose or eyes, should not bathe just after a meal.

Phlegm patients should exercise substantially, and strong people and those who eat fatty food, should exercise more during winter and spring. The body becomes firm and effective through correct exercise. However do not overdo things, believing it to be more effective. That is exaggerating and may work against you.

2. Secular Actions :

To live according to the moral code of the world is the basis for all good qualities.

Always keep your promise, return friendliness and obligations to others according to your word. However, if you have promised to keep word based on a bad action, you should abstain from such a word, while noble deeds should be followed right through, even if others try to prevent you from doing so.

Take care of your relatives and your workers with love. Remember for a long time others' kindness to you. Offer your service with respect to your parents, your advisor and the elders in the family. Let your thoughts be on a level with your friends, relatives and others you are in contact with.

Be moderate in your daily tasks, but give liberally when necessary. If you are wrong, admit it quickly. If you are right, or have achieved well at something, be content with that and do not dwell on it. You know perfectly well how you would react to others' boasting.

If you are knowledgeable, suppress your pride, and if you are rich, be content with that. Today, there are rich people and companies that only have one wish – to increase the money pot.

Never listen to slander, and keep intimate revelations to yourself; but with those who love you and those you trust completely, you can talk freely. Always be mild and controlled, spontaneously friendly and happy. If you send out an adverse message, you invite that person to become an enemy.

Never use words of deceit! You may get an enemy. Or, on reflection, you may get a gnawing remorse. Recognise it? It happens to most of us, but should be a lesson – "I will not do that again."

Never give your enemies an opening, but wait till time is ripe and fight them with good means. This is important enough to repeat.

Never show contempt regarding those working for you, and avoid being envious of those above you. A good working climate is healthy.

Never deprive anyone of their wealth, because what harm you bestow on others, will reflect back on you. Never debase yourself to curse, even in trivial matters. Be gentle in all situations, so you have nothing to regret later. Never entrust power to evil people.

Wind people are impatient, and hate to wait till the time is right.

Bile anger gives wrong decisions, and Phlegm laziness or hesitation may wait till time is over-ripe.

Do not be too rash. Before you act, you should judge the situation, and then do properly, what is good and right.

Never accept a lot of assumptions as true, only accept them after judging them carefully. If you are stressed, you may quickly swallow the assumption as true. That is a Wind reaction.

If you are angry, you react without thinking; that is a Bile reaction, often coupled with Wind. Whatever you feel in your heart yourself. First express it inwardly, and then put words to the main points.

That is – avoid Wind, Bile or Wind+Bile reactions! Judging the situation includes Phlegm, as you quieten down, and that will balance the Wind and/or the Bile. But don't hesitate too long! Then you may "miss the boat" – that is Phlegm in imbalance.

You see, the philosophy of Wind, Bile and Phlegm is so logical, in all ways of life.

So, apply this for the following advices, too!

3. Holy Actions:

Since all of us hunger for joy, we engage in all sorts of activities. But if we do not practise the good teachings, our joy will be contaminated and become a source of suffering. Therefore, we should strive to live and practise the good, and avoid negative and evil people.

In body, speech and mind you should refrain from the ten negations:

To take life,
to steal,
to partake in sexual misconduct,
to lie,
to slander,
use harsh talk,
be confrontational in talk,
to lust,
show malice, and
express distorted views.

A Norwegian doctor exclaimed at a seminar: *Every one of us should stick this advice to the wall, read it daily and follow it. This is the best advice I have ever seen!*

B. *Seasonal lifestyles*:

If the disturbance is of cold Phlegm that has arisen during winter, the cleansing should be done in spring.

Wind disturbances that have arisen during summer should be cleansed in the autumn.

Bile disturbances that have built up in the autumn should be cleansed in late autumn.

Such cleansing should be in co-operation with a doctor/ natural doctor.

C. *Impulses*:

Do not go against the following impulses:

Hunger,
thirst,
vomiting,
yawning,
sneezing,

breathing,
sleep,
removing mucus from the lungs (light cough)
saliva,
faeces,
air in the intestines,
urine,
semen.

Of course suppressing an impulse from time to time can be forgiven! But if it becomes a habit to force back the natural impulses of the body, or force them forward, all kinds of disturbances can arise and become chronic, and the five Winds will immediately suffer. Adjust diet, drink and medicines as for Wind diseases.

To *deter from food* regularly, obviously leads to physical breakdown, weakness and dizziness.

To counteract this tendency, one should use light, oily food with hot potency in small amounts.

If you *deny yourself drink* regularly, dryness develops in the mouth, and could result in dizziness, heart problems and confusion.

Here all cooling factors are favourable to restore the balance. Most people do not drink enough, or drink coke and the like. What is wrong with water, the purest of all?

To *force back the need to vomit,* can lead to anorexia, asthma, and the first stage in epilepsy, erysipelas, skin itching, boils, eye illnesses, mucus and contagious disturbances.

Fasting may help, inhaling the strong smoke from Tibetan incense or rinsing the mouth with a decoction of sandalwood.

To *force back the want to sneeze* as a habit, dulls the sense organs, leads to headaches, stiff neck, corners of the mouth pointing downward and fracture of the jawbone because of Wind disturbances.

Inhaling incense as above, taking Tibetan medicines for the nose and looking at the sun may cure this.

To *force back the need to yawn,* can lead to problems equivalent to sneezing, and the ways to treat Wind problems.

To *force back gasping for breath* when you are exhausted or after hard exercise, can induce tumours, heart diseases and confusion.

It is necessary to rest, and only then, this treatment for Wind problems will be favourable.

To *deny oneself sleep,* increases the need to yawn, increases tiredness, the head becomes heavy, one gets digestive problems and can develop even cataract.

Drink warm milk, or meat soup, in the evening. Oil massage might help, or a drop of lukewarm sesame oil in the ears.

When one *does not clear the throat of mucus,* the mucus will accumulate, and can lead to asthma, weight loss, hiccups, heart problems and congestion in the gullet (oesophagus). Get rid of the mucus using wild ginger and long pepper.

To *force back saliva* can give pains in the heart and the head, loss of liquid through the nostrils, dizziness and congestion of the gullet.

To *force back air* in the intestines, results in dry faeces, constipation, difficulties in passing wind, tumours, shooting pains in the womb, feeble sight, reduced body heat and heart problems.

To *hold back when you need to pass faeces,* forces the residues upwards instead of downwards! This gives headaches, displacements in the muscles of the large intestine, influenza and the same symptoms as for retained wind. It is so toxic to the body, that if it becomes a habit, it can lead to cancer.

To *force back the need to urinate,* can lead to kidney grit, disturbances in the bladder/urinary tract, in the male genital organs, hips, and the same symptoms as for suppressed wind.

Suppositories may help, and medicinal baths, wet fomentation, oil massage, steam and medicinal butter. (All this involves Tibetan medicines/oils). Even if fasting or other soothing methods can ease problems like these, remnants of the problems may reappear. Only enema, i.e., full cleansing of the intestines, and emetics, can prevent the problems reappearing.

So, whether it concerns faeces or urine – don't delay going to the toilet, because it is inconvenient. "I haven't got the time just now". Oh, really?

To *force back the emptying of semen* leads to unintentional discharge of semen, disturbances in the genital organs, disturbances in passing urine, increased formation of grit and may lead to operative removal of the outer male genital organs.

Suppositories and wet fomentation as above can help, normal copulation, the use of sesame oil, milk, chicken meat, and for a very short spell, alcohol.

Check board: The art of life

A symbol of offering of the five senses.
Consists of the mirror: Vision and Karma. Flower : Touch. Fruit: Taste. Smelling conch: Purge. Brass cymbals draped in skill cloth: Sound. Bronze vessel: Space

You must see the potential in developing a loving form of patience,
a tolerance based on courage, not on pessimism.
Tolerance and patience are not signs of failure, but of victory.
As you daily learn more patience, more tolerance with wisdom and
courage, you will see that this is the true source of success.
And actually, if you are too impatient, that is failure.

H.H. the Dalai Lama

The endless knot: Love and abandonment.

Chapter - III
TIBETAN DIAGNOSIS

Through an accurate diagnosis a Tibetan doctor can trace the illness back to its original source, the root of chronic illnesses may stem from years back.

The Tibetan doctor must consider

psychological factors,
climate,
age,
individual constitution, and
diet.

Psychological factors:

Basis for the diagnosis is Wind, Bile and Phlegm. You know enough about them now, to say. Of course, that is what is at the core of the diagnosis.

The balance among these three energies maintains the relation between body and mind, and their connection with the environment. When the energies are too weak, too strong or damaged, they may develop into a too hot, too cold or both too hot and cold illness.

The doctor studies the five sense organs: Eyes, ears, nose, tongue and skin and their relative sensitiveness, plus saliva, faeces, urine, vomit and blood when needed.

Climate:

Different environments have different influences on body and mind. You easily recognize that when you go on the mountains, or feel jetlag.

A cold, dry, very windy living place can be a strong added cause to a Wind illness. A very hot and dry climate can worsen a Bile illness, and a cold and humid climate a Phlegm illness.

The cold and dry winter increases Wind-symptoms, the hot summer weather increases Bile, especially if it is not humid, and cold and humid weather increases Phlegm illnesses.

The Wind patient might feel better moving to a less windy spot – he is not an island man. The Bile patient may seek boat-life or mountain-life in the summer season. However, the Phlegm patient will want to flee the winter. As do some Wind people too. Pensioners who flee to Florida are elderly people who often suffer from cold Wind problems – remember that Wind is more prevalent in elderly people.

Wind symptoms are worst at daybreak and sunset, Bile at midday and midnight, and Phlegm morning and evening.

The Tibetans talk of six seasons, and each of the seasons influence its own special organ. For instance, the heart is influenced by summer heat, while the kidneys are influenced by the winter cold.

You are sensitive to the changes in the weather, and when the moon is new or full. Many people do not know that the moon influences us. It is so logical, though. Our bodies consist of 60-70% liquid, so it is not only the sea that has ebb and flood! In some European countries, doctors are actually reluctant to operate when there is a full moon – unless there is an emergency. The "flood" in the blood may result in excess bleeding.

Age:

Age is influenced by the three temperaments. A child is a Phlegm type, from the teens till about 60 is the Bile type, while the old person is Wind type – increasingly so with age.

This also means that in old age, you might be more liable to get a Wind imbalance, if you are a Wind person.

In the same way, Phlegm imbalances may be stronger in childhood – which you for instance often find with asthma, and Bile imbalances in your "Bile age".

The individual constitution:

Just as important is the personal type – male, female or neutral (as mentioned before, independent of being a male or female person), the individual constitution is an important factor.

Whether thin or fat, the bone structure, posture, skin colour, being drowsy, talkative, etc.

Wind symptoms usually turn up in the lower part: hips, pelvis and the legs, bile in the middle part, liver and gall bladder, and Phlegm in the upper part, in the brain and arms.

Diet:

If the complaints are worse just after the meal, Phlegm is involved. If worse when the food is digested, Bile is involved. When hunger is gnawing before the meal, Wind is involved. The doctor is interested in the following specific symptoms.

Wind-symptoms:

Yawning,
shivering,
sighing,
the need to stretch,
shivering with cold,
pain in the hips, waist, bones, joints. Pains that move around are typical, one day the pain is here, the other day there.

Avoid underdone meat, pork, dry food such as biscuits and cookies and tea. Nourishing food is important. The same is heat, and close friends. Of course – close friends are warm, aren't they!

Bile symptoms:

Bitter taste in the mouth,
recurrent headaches,
surface fever,
acute pain in the upper part of the body,
digestive pains.

Avoid hot and strongly spiced food (cannot be repeated often enough), strong energetic actions, and sitting in the sun.

Concentrate on cool food – yoghurt is a good example, and fresh salads. Plus finding a cool spot.

Phlegm symptoms:

Loss of appetite,
the sense of having a full stomach even without eating,
frequent vomiting,
frequent belching,
digestive problems,
discomfort after having eaten,
poor sense of taste,
cold or heavy in body and mind.

Avoid heavy, fatty food, and sitting or lying on the ground. Use warm food, warm clothes, and enjoy the sun and the fireside.

If we put all these many factors together, the doctor has a good starting-point for a real diagnosis. We have seen results from these diagnoses that have been more precise than Western medical examinations with all its apparatus – amazing as it is. And quick too!

A Tibetan doctor is always the first to emphasise that the combinations of Western and Tibetan diagnosis can be helpful or necessary.

The doctor considers the patient's height, build, age, the colour of the conjunctiva of the eyes (i.e., the membrane which covers the front of the eyeball and the inside of the eyelids), saliva, faeces, skin damage, and specifically – ears, tongue, and urine.

If the patient is weak, pale, thin (and small), he has a Wind-constitution. If the patient is of medium height, with a light skin, and sweats a lot, he has a Bile constitution. If the patient has a swollen face, and an upright walk, he has a Phlegm constitution.

Eye diagnosis:

If the whites of the eyes are reddish, this indicates a Wind symptom.

If the look is stiff and focused on one point, this is a very serious Wind symptom, and can also be due to damage in the brain cells.

If the whites of the eyes are yellowish, or the veins are noticeable, this indicates a Bile symptom.

If the whites of the eyes are yellowish red, it indicates fever or something the matter with the blood.

If the sight is weak and the colour pale, this indicates a Phlegm symptom.

If the eyes are strongly red, this can be due to impure blood.

Enlarged pupils indicate poisoning or damaged brain cells.

If the whites of the eye of a child are yellowish red, it may indicate measles. If the eyes are turned upwards, liver energy is low.

If the eyelids are swollen, it indicates oedemas or a weak kidney function.

If the front part of the eyelids is pale, this indicates anaemia. Red eyelids indicate disturbances in the blood; yellow eyelids indicate Bile disturbances and whitish pale eyelids Phlegm disturbances.

Ear diagnosis:

This is especially used for babies and small children. At the back of the ear three veins are placed above each other. The ear of the child is examined from the back by letting the (sun) light fall on the front, so that light shines through. If the vein is clear, thin, straight and with few branches, this is a healthy sign.

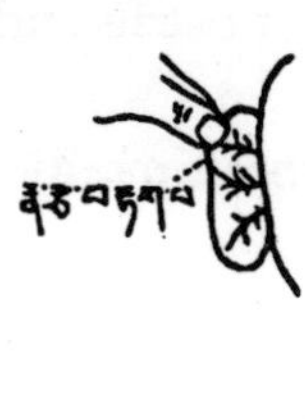

The upper indicates the lungs. Right ear for a boy, left ear for a girl. The upper left ear of a boy represents the heart, and the right ear of a girl likewise.

The middle vein on the right ear represents the liver, and on the left ear the spleen.

The lower vein on the right side indicates the right kidney and on the left side, the left kidney.

If the "lung" vein is dark, filled and thick, this indicates a lung inflammation. If it is pale coloured, this indicates a Wind defect connected with the mother/child relationship. If it is yellowish pale, it indicates a cold disease in the lungs.

If the "spleen" vein is thick, dark, and filled, this indicates a warm inflammatory illness in stomach and spleen. If the colour is yellowish pale, it indicates a cold disease in stomach or spleen.

If the right "kidney" vein is filled, thick and dark coloured, there is an inflammation in the right kidney or urinary bladder. Inflammations are otherwise always of a warm character. If the vein is yellowish pale, the child has a cold illness. The left "kidney" vein is parallel to the right vein.

If the "heart" vein is filled, thick and dark coloured, this indicates a heart inflammation. If the colour is yellowish pale, there is a cold illness in the heart.

If the "liver" vein is filled, thick and dark, there is inflammation in the liver. If the colour is yellowish pale, it is a cold disease.

Nose Diagnosis:

The energy of the lungs or the heart is weak if there is a crack in the nose.

Irritated or runny nose indicates a cold illness, influenza or allergy.

Blocked nose or dry nostrils indicates inflammation in the lungs.

A dark spot on the nose tip indicates stomach problems.

Frequent sneezing and inflamed nose phlegm may indicate a chronic problem.

Tongue diagnosis:

This is one of the more important visual diagnoses, especially for Wind diseases that have arisen after a long, successful treatment of fever or a warm illness.

If the tongue is red, coarse and too dry, it is a *Wind* symptom. If it is dry, pale and weak, this indicates in addition a warm disturbance or fever.

If the tongue is dry and dark coloured, this indicates equal parts of *Wind and fever.*

If the tongue is brownish yellow and there is a bitter taste, it indicates *Bile* disturbances. If the tongue is smooth, dry and stiff, it indicates *Wind + Bile.*

If the tongue is watery, pale, soft, with a sticky, grey coating, it indicates a *Phlegm* disturbance.

If there is a thick fatty coating on the tongue, it indicates *Phlegm* (too much phlegm) in the stomach and liver.

If the tongue is pale and has a thick grey coating, it indicates spread and complicated *fever.* A pale tongue with small red "pimples" indicates unripe fever. If the tongue is dry, stiff and with a bitter taste, it is acute fever.

If there is a crack in the middle part of the tongue, this is to do with *the heart.*

If the tongue is pale and the lips at the same time dark, there is an inflammation in *the spleen.*

If both sides of the tongue are dark, there is a problem with *the kidneys.*

If the tip of the tongue is brown and cracked, it indicates a complex stomach and liver disturbance where Wind, Bile and Phlegm are all involved.

If there is a swelling under the tongue and it is difficult to talk and eat, this indicates a too strong growth of *tongue tissue.*

If the tongue is swollen and liquid flows from the mouth, and it is difficult to eat, the problem is the tongue itself.

Urine diagnosis:

This is the most important among the visual forms of diagnosis, and is used together with pulse diagnosis (see below) in many consultations. Urine diagnosis is difficult to practise, but fascinating.

Wind, Bile and Phlegm give us, as mentioned before, strong associations to the Greek temperaments (sanguine, choleric, phlegmatic). The impulses came indirectly from Greece, in the eighth century, with the Persian doctor who stayed for a longer period in Tibet, when they had symposiums in Tibet with doctors also from India, China and Mongolia. Quite advanced!

The urine diagnosis too, came to Tibet from Greece, probably with the Persian doctor. Today, however, urine diagnosis seems to be practised in Tibetan medicine *only*. It ought to be known and used world wide, as it can give unprecedented quick and clear information!

If the patient cannot come to the doctor, an experienced doctor may give a diagnosis within a day on the basis of fresh urine sample alone, without even seeing the patient.

The doctor preferably examines fresh, still warm urine. He studies

its colour,
smell,
bubbles,
cloudiness or steam,
sediments, creaminess and
"clouds",
often using a small stick to stir the urine.

The doctor firstly examines fresh urine. In the West, you rarely get that, but you do get that morning's urine. The doctor studies when and how the urine changes, and its characteristics during the change. He may also diagnose quite a lot from a sample of urine that is days old.

If by now, you think that you know enough to make your own diagnosis – think again! It is definitely much more complicated than you think. One single sign may catch your eye, and you may think – that's it! Don't. You may scare yourself and others, and may be completely wrong! You need the *whole* picture, and to have that, you must be an experienced Tibetan doctor.

In Tibet one could always find where the doctor resided, as there was usually a heap of cow horns outside. They had been used as containers for the urine samples.

At a seminar in Oslo anonymous urine samples were analysed by Dr. Lobsang Wangyal. The "patients" were healthy homeopathic students, but one sample was special after all. "This is the urine of a woman", said Dr. Wangyal, "she is pregnant in her third week, and otherwise healthy". She was!

Another participant – the only one who was not a student – had very dark and ill smelling urine, so even we, who were not versed in urine diagnosis, could see that something was wrong. However, Dr. Wangyal discretely did not give this verdict in public. It was too serious for that. The young man had liver and heart problems, Dr. Wangyal told me afterwards. He told the young man to seek a heart specialist, and shortly afterwards he had a successful by-pass.

A simple test – shake the glass with urine and hold it close to the ear. If it fizzes, it *might* indicate infection. If, for instance, we consider urine that is transparent, watery in colour, with large bubbles in a moderate amount that appear immediately when the urine is stirred, this indicates a Wind illness, Dr. Wangyal explained – as the bubbles are few and disappear so quickly, it clearly shows an inflammation. Clinically there are two areas that normally correspond to these characteristics – the stomach and the kidneys. But in this case it cannot be the stomach, because the diluted and watery urine and the few bubbles immediately indicate a case of kidney. This is because although both the organs are Phlegm areas, the kidney is a fluid-organ, while the stomach is a solid Phlegm organ. The conclusion must be inflammation of the kidneys.

Clear to him, but not at all to me. But I understood this much. What an instrument the urine analysis is for diagnosis! Quick and reliable for a trained doctor. Without any cumbersome analysis or apparatus used on the patient. A Western analysis may take days to give you an answer.

There are certain rules for what one can eat and drink, and for the intake of medicines the day before the morning urine is taken. Some patients forget that, and are very much surprised when the doctor reveals that they have been taking medicines the previous day. Or even just vitamin pills.

Dr. Wangyal showed me that the Wind urine is watery bluish, the Bile urine reddish yellow, with much steam and a strong, stale smell. The Phlegm urine is mostly clear as water, but could also be white as milk. I found it very difficult to interpret; I felt colour blind!

The doctor recognises the hot and cold illness through the urine analysis. Plus Wind, Bile and Phlegm and their combinations, poisoning, whether the patient has a cold or an influenza, intestinal colic, weak or poor digestion, much air in the stomach, inflammation of mucous membranes in the intestines, liver inflammation, lung inflammation, bronchitis, asthma, functional heart disease, rheumatic heart disease, anaemia, meningitis, just to mention a few!

Pulse diagnosis:

Generally the Tibetan doctor uses the same principles as in Chinese pulse diagnosis. There are a few differences, though.

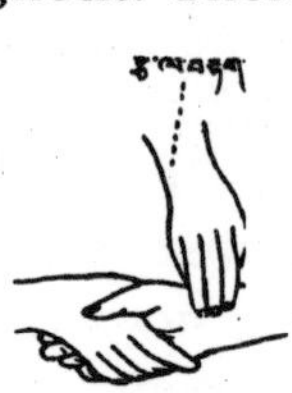

Learning to interpret the pulses correctly is very complicated and needs long experience. In the Tibetan medical study pulse diagnosis alone takes one whole year – and it takes ten years of experience to become a really proficient diagnostician. Thus it is very complicated to explain pulse diagnosis, however, here I try somehow.

On each wrist there are three positions for the inner organs. The doctors "read" the patient's pulse, including interpreting the functioning of the six vital organs – lung, heart, spleen, liver and kidneys, and of the six hollow organs: Stomach, small and large intestine, bile bladder, urinary bladder and the reproductive organs. He reads it with a light pressure of the index finger, a deeper pressure of the middle finger and a still deeper pressure with the ring finger.

In addition the patient's inherent character is studied – whether male, female or neutral. As mentioned before, these characters are independent of the person being male or female. Then Wind, Bile and Phlegm and their combinations are studied, cold, hot and combined cold/ hot, whether the illness is acute or chronic.

The pulses of the seasons and the day, and whether the elements have a detrimental or revitalising effect which we can illustrate with a symbolic example – if the Water element comes before the Fire element, there may be too little Fire (water quenches fire), i.e., too low Bile (heat) energy.

The Wind pulse yields easily to pressure, has little resilience, can have an irregular rhythm and skips some beats. The Bile pulse fast, taut, full, tight and strong. The Phlegm pulse weak, slow, sunken, gives easily to pressure.

The Tibetan doctors can also diagnose the death pulse early, and many other specific pulses, e.g., within psychiatry.

If you wonder at the skill of Tibetan diagnosis, you will be inspired by this special case history:

This story is from the American hospital Yale-Haven. It took the Western doctors a long time and many expensive examinations to find out what was wrong with a lady – a difficult diagnosis. So to test on the reliability of Tibetan diagnosis, Dr. Donden was told nothing in advance, about what was wrong with the patient. Only one of the doctors at the hospital knew the real diagnosis. The report is from one of the American doctors present at the examination, Dr. Selzer:

> The patient was awakened early, and told she would be examined by a Tibetan doctor, and asked to submit a urine sample. For her this was only one of an endless row of tests and examinations. Dr. Yeshi Donden in his monk's garbs went forward to the patient alone. There were no outer signs of what was wrong with the lady in the hospital bed. The Tibetan doctor studied her for a long while, bent over her, held her wrists between his hands. For half an hour he stood like that, listening with a bent head and closed eyes, silent. All his power seemed to be drawn towards this task. It was as if he and the patient were in their own sphere. From time to time the woman lifted her head and looked at the doctor. I wish I too could have been held like that. I have analysed a thousand pulses, but really have not sensed one... At long last Dr. Yeshi Donden straightened, put the woman's hand carefully down and retired a few steps. His assistant gave him a bowl with two sticks, Dr. Donden poured some of the urine from the woman in it, and then whipped it with the sticks. He then bent his head over the bowl and drew in the smell from the urine three times, put the bowl aside and turned to leave. Not a word had been said. But the woman lifted her head and said in an earnest voice: "Thank you so much, doctor" – and moved the hand he had held. The doctor turned and looked at her before he left.
>
> In the conference room he spoke for the first time: He talked about winds that flooded through the body of the woman, floods which broke towards barriers and ended in a creek, in a whirlpool. These whirls are in her blood, he said. Between her heart's chambers there had, before she was born, blown a wind which had opened a deep gate which should never have been open. Through this the waters flooded in her river, like a mountain brook in strong spring roar hit against and hammered loose from the riverbed, tearing with it fragments from the riverbed and flooding the breath – Dr. Donden said no more. Only then did the professor of the hospital disclose the diagnosis: An inborn heart disease. She had an opening between the heart chambers with heart failure as result. Inoperable. Indeed! A gate in the heart that

> should never have been opened. Through it floods the water that overflows the breath.
> This is a doctor who listens to the sounds of the body, for which we others are deaf. He is more than a doctor. He is a priest.

Another example:

> GEOFF, three years old, had a high fever, a strong headache and double vision. Several allopathic doctors were consulted, including some neurologists. The poor boy underwent a wide range of tests, but nothing was found. He became very thin and weak, and his parents feared for his life. After consulting a Tibetan doctor his headache and double vision were cured within weeks! It was found that the poor boy suffered from combined meningitis and tuberculosis – strangely not discovered by any of the allopathic doctors the family consulted. Now the boy is as healthy as any child.

Mountains and sea: Earth and Water elements as used in carpet designs. The garuda - a mythical bird, with many interpretations.

One being, the remover of obstacles and illnesses.

Patience has many interpretations:
One must have endless patience not to build up a feeling of hatred.
But some are of the opinion that patience means passivity, and that
one should act before something happens.
If someone does something wrong, you should take your precautions.
That is quite necessary, but do it without losing your mental peace.
Then you are still in a patient state. While you act.

H. H. the Dalai Lama

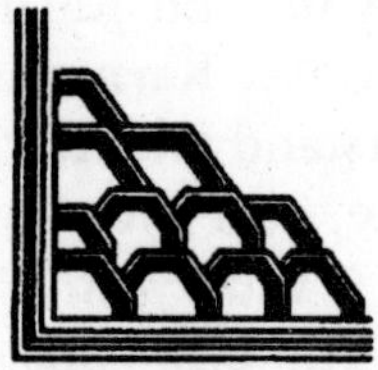

The mountain - a symbol of Earth

Chapter - IV

TIBETAN PSYCHIATRY

The understanding of the human mind that forms the basis for the Tibetan psychiatry in the seventh-eighth centuries, only began to dawn in the West in the eighteenth century!

As has been mentioned initially, Tibetan medicine is primarily a psychological religion, and the core of the teaching of Buddha is that mind is the base for all phenomena. Through your mind you create health as well as illness. Your mind is much stronger than you think! Positive thinking is a strong medicine, while negative thinking eventually results in illness.

The psychiatry is, just as physical illness, understood through the three temperaments and the three defects:

Wind is caused by desire,
Bile is caused by aversion, hate and anger,
Phlegm is caused by delusion.

Tibetan medicine calculates with five main causes for psychiatric problems, including insanity:

Karma,
defects of Wind, Bile and Phlegm,
poison,
unstable emotions, and
unseen forces ("ghosts").

Karma is the ripening of what you have already done. In the West we wrongly interpret Karma as "fate", but fate is something directing you, and Karma is what you direct, through what you choose. Karma is not predetermined, which is how we understand fate. Karma is cause and effect. The choices you make, and the way you act is cause, the seed, while the effect is what your choices or your actions lead to, the ripening. The past consists of old choices, and you cannot do anything more about them.

All the time you shape your Karma from where you are just at that moment. The results from a choice are shaped by whatever you choose just now. All the time it is what you do now, which shapes your future. The future is the effect of what your choice of the moment has caused.

What does that really mean? It means that you have the possibility of developing a positive Karma all the time!

> A young friend, a gardener with a new nursery, had a prolapsed disk, went to the local hospital and insisted on an immediate operation – his choice. Perhaps he should have been less hasty (less Wind), and first found out where to have the operation. The operation unfortunately was unsuccessful – the effect of his choice to have the operation at the local hospital immediately. The doctors did not dare risk a second operation, neither locally nor at a specialized hospital, and the damaged nerves, now gave him added pain, that could not be repaired. I recommended the young man should try moxa treatment to ease his back and his pain, but he did not want to. Though it was worth a try, as it might have helped, and if not, no harm would be done. However, his lack of choice has resulted in constant pain, and he is unable to work. That is his Karma!

However, we are also ruled by ignorance – of not understanding. And in the West our ignorance is often ruled by stress. This is a kind of madness. By having a lot of thoughts in your head, and things happening all the time, you flee from your real choices.

You find the real choices by seeking silence, the stillness within yourself.

Compare yourself to a glass of impure water. If you move it all the time, all the water stays impure. If you leave it alone, the impurities sink to the bottom, and you can enjoy the pure water (mind). But we act as if silence is our enemy, and not our best friend!

There is also a collective karma – politically, culturally, and socially.

Whatever you choose, things happen according to that, and that is cause and effect. That is why karma is part of the responsibility of any illness in its deepest sense, because the lifestyle builds up to a logical eruption. Choosing to overindulge in tomatoes, or chocolate and cakes, or milk, or alcohol, or heavy smoking, result in illness. Often triggered by stress. The mind makes the wrong choice, and you choose to remain ignorant of what causes your "overindulgence".

As a whole, illness results from a lack of understanding the phenomena, not realising the principle of cause and effect, confining it only within the standpoint of our personal character.

The *insanity* arises when your pattern of life collides with your deepest character and insight. If the illness is entirely stemming from karma, it may be difficult to treat. Then it may not appear as an organic illness, and cannot be treated with medicines. That type of insanity can be cured, though, through the Dharmic medicine, where high ranking lama doctors with their special insight, can find the sources back in time which have caused the present insanity. For instance, it could easily have its source in early childhood, or just a forgotten incident that has a grip on your mind – a trauma.

The way the lama doctor works is different from the Western approach, but you can compare him with a psychiatrist – an excellent Tibetan version with its different approach.

Defects of Wind:

Physical, mental and emotional stress. This is part of what increases Wind. When you are too intense in discussion and brain work, constantly worrying about what has not been finished, aims that are too difficult to reach, constant worry over family problems, when you overreact to something you have lost – be it a person close to you or material things, excessive lusts – of material things, food, sex or a fanatic interest.

Symptoms of such emotional disturbances are varied. The person is nervous and agitated, apologetic, or the mouth is too busy talking about anything that pops up. He does not remember what has been said, cannot concentrate or finish something he has started. The chaos in him is a blockage.

He weeps for nothing, or suddenly rages for nothing, or is restless, anxious and highly-strung. This leads to wrong reactions that make the problems worse. He loses appetite, or eats too much of one thing – a fanatic addiction. He becomes sleepless – sleeplessness is a typical Wind suffering. The eyes become red and blurry, and worse after eating. Hands and legs shiver, the knees feel stiff, and he flinches suddenly. Being too nervous and agitated, his movements are too quick, and that makes him accident-prone.

Treatment: Concentration should be first on diet and then behaviour. Fatty foods reduces Wind, so do regular meals and regular sleep.

He needs a warm beautiful room, which is not too light – the lighter, the more Wind. Fill the room with a mass of flowers. Loving care from family and friends is an excellent medicine.

When Wind persons love something, like harmonious music, or reading, this can open up ways for further treatment, such as talk therapy. (Mozart and Bach should be part of any hospital treatment!)

One can also use acupuncture with needles of gold on specific psychological acupuncture points, gold hammer acupuncture or moxa treatment. Gold is tranquillising.

In Tibetan Yoga medicine, singing bowls may be used.

Defects of Bile:

This is part of what increases Bile: Bile based physical imbalance may turn into mental disturbances with symptoms of violence and roughness. Where there is anger, hate and aversion there is an over production of bile. Alcohol, coffee, tobacco, strongly spiced food are Bile stimulating. The physical, organic part of the Bile imbalance (defects) may include special physiological skin problems, heart-blood vessel and stomach-intestine symptoms, that are clear parallels to modern psychiatric classification.

He has a sharp tongue, swears, and is rough handed, smashing things; he can hurt and kill in anger. This is because he is constantly angry and intense, never forgetting what has angered him in the past.

The skin is yellowish, the lachrymal fluid yellow, and he sees stars in front of his eyes.

Treatment: A Tibetan doctor, who by vocation is compassionate and warm, may find it necessary to treat the Bile patient harshly. This patient must avoid all Bile stimulating food and drink, such as fatty foods, eggs and not least, hot spices and alcohol. The best environments are cool places and to stay by the sea or in the mountains, in rooms with cool colours like blue and sea green. In addition the patient should have herbal medicines and special medicinal baths.

Defects of Phlegm:

This is part of what disturbs Phlegm: Disturbances increase through confusion, ignorance and dullness. The Phlegmatic mentally ill person withdraws totally, becomes silent, sulky and passive, sleeps too much, refusing to eat. The eyes have a tendency to roll upwards; he is clammy and has fits of fainting. He forgets where he has put things. The joints can be swollen; the nose drips, and saliva may drip from the mouth.

Treatment: Much love and care is needed for the mentally disturbed Phlegm person. It is important to encourage him to do something, and he needs a lot of exercise.

Physiotherapy will do him well, but it must contain massage, as well as physical exercises, and heat stimulation. Certainly not the mechanical type of massage you can sometimes get. Reassuring hands doing massage is real therapy!

A warm and light room, with warm colours, will also ease him, together with friends and warm words.

Diet should be adjusted to fight Phlegm – as much boiled food as possible, not raw, cold or fried. He should avoid sweet things, fat, milk, butter, and cold drinks. A good diet should include coarse-grained flour, vegetables and starch.

Herbal medicines and warm medicinal baths will do him good, and medicinal butter when it is necessary to incite vomiting.

Wind is equivalent to classical schizophrenia, characteristic disturbances in the way of thinking, spirit of mind and behaviour.

Phlegm is equivalent to the catatonic type that is retired schizophrenia, generally inhibited, mute, dull, negative or "violent-soft". Some cases end in a purely vegetative condition.

Violent Bile is equivalent to schizophrenia of the catatonic type. The patient is agitated, marked by exaggerated and sometimes violent motor activity and excitement.

Poison can trigger insanity directly, due to poisons in the environment – not unusually at work, with strong chemicals acquired over a length of time, strong medication that is not tolerated, or narcotics.

The poisoning may be due to one special poison, or the wrong combination of otherwise innocent food, drink and medicines (such as hot spices and alcohol in a Bile case). Even mild "poisons" can be detrimental, when accumulated over time.

The mind may be totally deranged, the body energy is sapped, and the face especially looks dead, losing its entire glow. The poison causes deep delusions; the patient does not know his own mind.

Here a regulation of diet does not help, as long as the poison remains in the body. This must first be driven out of the body through medicines.

When the feelings of sorrow/worry gnaw and gnaw, they become a fixed idea, and end in neuroses and psychoses (as for instance manic depressive, pathological cleanliness). There are three basic categories:

Fear and paranoia, which is *Wind*

Aggression, which is *Bile*

Depression and withdrawal, which is *Phlegm.*

If the cause is purely psychological, this will influence the life wind, which is directly coupled to the mind.

To lose something material, or to lose a beloved, may for many be a devastating experience – the job, the dwelling, status, parents, a child, and the wife/husband.

We panic, protest against our ill fortune, or refuse to acknowledge that the loss has happened. This leads to such a tension that the person may become schizophrenic.

To find that our ego or our actions or anything material does not have a lasting, constant worth, can be painful as well as frightening, and may lead to psychosis.

According to Buddhist philosophy, the psychological reason for mental disturbances is the same as for insight!.

If we work through the problems till we understand that nothing is permanent, constant, it will not only free us from mental disturbances, it will in addition deepen our understanding and strengthen our mental and spiritual mind. Well, even if we do not fully understand the Buddhist thought that nothing is permanent, (that may be a bit too vast to understand); at least it is indeed logical to understand that clinging to what is no more, is in vain and destructive, and by realising that, we feel released.

The way to treat overwhelming sorrow and worry, is through diet and herbal medicines, adjusted to the imbalance of Wind, Bile or Phlegm, change in your lifestyle, meditation and awakening of consciousness.

Lama doctors also treat psychoses and extreme cases of illness.

Demons, evil spirits. What Tibetan philosophy means by this, a Yoga teacher taught his pupil in the 12th century:

"... A demon is very, very large, and totally black. Any one seeing such a being truly becomes scared and shivers from head to foot. But in reality the demons do not *exist!*"

Tibetan philosophy (psychology if you like) says, whatever prevents you from attaining freedom is a demon.

Even caring and loving parents can be demons if they prevent your independent way.

But the largest demon of all is the belief in Self as an independent and lasting principle. If you cannot destroy this clinging to Self, the demons will continue to encourage you – and destroy you.

The ordinary man or woman may fully believe that these outer, negative forces really are demons, but Tibetan philosophy considers them as mental entities or projections, or as psychic energy fields. When such a force overcomes a person, it takes over and expresses itself through body, speech and mind. The reason for it being able to take over and penetrate through the conscious psyche is that the person is psychically weak and does not have any power of resistance.

Mostly, what are here called "demons" are not seen entities or ghosts, but only a mental attitude going into the extreme, or a mental attitude which dictates your feelings and actions.

It could be a trauma. From childhood, from being misused and "forgetting" it, or other situations, which are too difficult to accept.

Or as mentioned above, your well-meaning parents who "guide" you may be your demons, guiding you contrary to your own deep wishes. If the father is a lawyer, there is a tradition that the child shall continue on that path – even though it is contrary to his true nature. The same in business.

Perhaps that is why the third generation often is the weakest link, not running the business successfully.

A misinterpreted ambition can also lead to disaster. You achieved so well at school, that you could study medicine – being a doctor gives prestige and money. These are two demons – one is greed, the other, self pride. But you will not be a good doctor if your soul is not in it. That may be the reason, why some doctors become addicted to narcotics, for instance, or become very authoritative, not listening to others, and definitely not to the patient – "I know the best!" They did not have a genuine calling.

Other demons are – extreme sexual activity, extreme laziness, and extreme greed.

Also after being brainwashed you are guided by a demon to become a terrorist, or a religious maniac. Hatred is getting rooted and is ruling. Fanaticism is demonic. Just think of the sects that encourage mass suicide! The psychopath is a demon. He is brainwashing too. Making you believe you are no good. If you are over sensitive, you are especially vulnerable. Demonic classmates may bully a child at school !

Invisible demons eat away – this is how Tibetan psychiatry explains anorexia.

And bulimia. Hungry demons with big inflated stomachs and thin, dry throats, voracious for food and drink.

You become ruled by thoughts and habits contrary to your true nature – they build up till you are caught by the "demon", i.e., the negative forces. These are dark forces within you, too dark to bring into your conscious mind. As long as they can gnaw away inside you, the demons will rule. You may become physically ill as well as mentally ill. Often it can be karmic based.

The ego-clutching big demon is the cause of all damage, fear and pain in the world. Tibetan lamas express that a demon is like a coagulation of energies that are too compact.

Sometimes a patient suddenly changes his behaviour, e.g., suddenly becoming an alcoholic, often shows symptoms of a demon being present. How he behaves, is dependent on which type of demon, that is, which type of psychosis, he is guided by. Tibetan psychiatric medicine has here a detailed and very old system of classifying demons, based on psychological and physical symptoms of behaviour.

The Tibetan doctor easily finds out whether you are ruled by a demon, through observing you, reading your pulses and a very special way of interpreting the urine, which will indicate what kind of demon is involved.

They might even find that there is something wrong with the ground you are living on – electro-magnetic fields, which are detrimental to your health, are "demons".

In all, the doctor classifies the demons into eighteen basic spirits. However, among the many demons, the Tibetans say there are really only two – those created from hope and those created from doubt. Both of them stem from basic ignorance that makes us believe in a permanent Self.

But nothing in this world is permanent.

The self is an illusion. This is the central theme in Tibetan Buddhism. The whole world is impermanent, transient; it is a dynamic manifestation of energies. Nothing is solid. Our bodies, our egos, the mountains, and the stars. Everything is a temporary form of tiny particles in endless flux.

The treatment is far ranging, but precise. And diet is important!

Diet is the first part of the cure. Next comes a complicated composition of herbal medicinal treatment. The Wind sufferer may also be helped by massage, the Bile sufferer through medicinal baths, the Phlegm sufferer will be given emetics, to vomit, and if Blood is involved, bloodletting is part of the cure.

In addition, when necessary, there are many specific anti demon techniques, through the Dharma medicine.

> ARNE, 25 years old, is a schizophrenic. He visits the Tibetan doctor, who says that the precious pills may help, but above all he benefits from the gold hammer acupuncture. He was not cured, but got more control.

Mrs. Simpson had been suffering depression that caused weakness in the right side of her body. It worsened and affected her speech. She consulted a Tibetan doctor after trying all sorts of allopathic and homeopathic treatment. With Tibetan medicines there was rapidly a marked improvement, concerning speech as well as the general depression.

We should take Tibetan psychiatry in earnest. H.H. the Dalai Lama participated in a symposium at Harvard University, together with several American professors in psychiatry, psychology, medical doctors, biochemists and others; and the conclusion from the Westerners on Tibetan medicine was – "... And we thought we in the West invented psychology! We are actually centuries behind, and have much to learn!"

In fact, Tibetan yogis can sit naked for hours in the snow during meditation, and not become cold. Swathed in icy cold wet blankets they sit there, the blankets dry on their bodies, and they just remain warm. This is quite contrary to modern medical science, which alleges that in the cold, bodies protect themselves by withdrawing the heat to the heart and the interior of the body, leaving the extremities cold. The Western scientists got permission from His Holiness the Dalai Lama to go to the Himalayas and verify and research this phenomenon.

The pearl entwined with a scarf is a symbol of good angury.
The parasol symbolises protection against all evil

We need no temples; we need no complicated philosophy.
Our own heart is our temple; my philosophy is love.

H.H. the Dalai Lama

*Aconitum**

Chapter - V

TIBETAN MEDICINE

The medicines are developed to re-establish the balance in cold and hot disturbances, and the balance of Wind, Bile, Phlegm and blood, in addition to the specific illness.

The herbs are chosen according to their hot and cold characteristics and the innate character of Wind, Bile and Phlegm, and also, from where they grow – to the north or the south, east or west, in sun or shadow, in humid or dry soil. The Himalaya and parts of Tibet are unique starting points for the raw material. Here is a wide spectrum of herbs, healthy strong plants in pure Himalayan air.

The region is also very rich in minerals and precious stones, used in some Tibetan medicines. Many precious stones are only to be found in the Tibetan environment. Unusual to us is their supply of coral. But the Himalaya is the youngest mountain range in the world. They came into existence when half a continent tore loose from Australia, sped north, collided and pushed up the sea bottom, including the corals.

In addition to the many herbal pills for daily use, prescribed by the Tibetan doctor, there are :

---

* From Dr. Dawa's book *A Clear Mirror of Tibetan Medicinal Plants.*

A saint used such a fan to revive the souls of the dead.

The Precious Pills

In Norway, they are popularly called "silk cushions", as each pill is wrapped in silk, each type in a different colour. The precious pills are carefully packed by hand, and encased in their individual little box, sealed and airtight. This way they may last for several years.

Precious pills are very purifying and balanced pills, taken usually only once every five to fourteen days. They contain many precious metals and stones too, and are very cleansing and detoxifying, excellent for chronic diseases and poisoning. They consist of many ingredients, up to 185! These composite medicines have a synergetic effect, i.e., the effect is bigger than the sum of the ingredients.

The Tibetans usually have at least two types of precious pills, in their home pharmacy, to be used as an antidote. One contains 35 ingredients, the other 70. In addition to the daily medicines, or – even as a follow-up medicine, to maintain stability, Precious Pills are really precious!

Tibetan medicine goes to the *root* of the problem – this can be a peeling off of symptoms that can last years. The peeling off may for instance start with blood or Bile, continue via Phlegm and end up with Wind. High blood pressure, for example, this is not one illness, but must be treated according to which defects are involved, and may need a peeling off. It will never be enough to tell a Tibetan doctor what ailment you have, and get the one medicine for that. There is no one medicine for an ailment; it all depends on what defect(s) are involved!

And no chronic illness consists of one illness alone. The treatment is like an onion, removing layer after layer. To restore imbalances acquired throughout many years, some years may pass to cure a chronic illness. A chronic disease has arisen after years of development in the wrong direction, perhaps even from birth or in the womb. May be inherited, too.

But no person is like another, one illness can have many causes, where one patient has this defect and another has other defects. In some the imbalance is simple and easy to correct, in others not. The weekly magazines have a tendency to present miracle stories, which give many patients sky high and unrealistic expectations. The third year Dr. Wangyal was here, he was interviewed on the radio, and we were swamped with telephone calls – some even years later. The interview gave no patients' histories, only went through the theories of cold, hot, temperaments and defects, and obviously gave many a feeling of "coming home". We only had the availability to supply appointments for a fraction of those who asked for one, and it was not easy to say "No" to that many.

Miracles take time. Though some are lucky and do experience a quick recovery, after having tried "everything".

For acute damage and acute illnesses, the Tibetan doctors recommend the medical attention of the West, but believe they can give better help regarding diverse chronic diseases. The main areas Tibetan medicine has focused on in the West are especially the many types of rheumatic sufferings and arthritis, allergies, skin diseases (eczema, atropic eczema, psoriasis, some vitiligo, etc.) asthma, chronic constipation, gastric ulcers, heart problems and spinal problems.

Some types of cancers can be cured or eased, and strengthening supportive therapy in cancer may be very effective. We have also seen some good results in supportive therapy for terminal cancer patients, such as one young woman who had insufferable pain and threw up whatever she ingested. The Tibetan medicines she was given, eased the pain, and she tolerated the food.

Diabetes too can also be helped, if not cured. We have also seen surprisingly good results in treatment of Parkinson's disease and in epilepsy. Gold hammer treatment and precious pills have been very helpful here. Also in treating Multiple Sclerosis.

Some case histories:

> Several years ago there was a chemical disaster at a factory in Bhopal in India, where 2500 people died, and thousands turned blind or got serious lung damage. The 200 Tibetans living in the surrounding area immediately took a *precious pill,* and not one of them died or suffered serious damage. They also distributed them to their neighbours, who also avoided the serious effects of the disaster.
>
> After the Chernobyl accident, Dr. Tenzin Choedrak tended to twenty patients in the hospital there, treating them with the precious pills Ratna Sampel and Rinchen Drangjor. Twelve were out of hospital within two weeks.
>
> A lady in her forties was gloriously happy. She had had atopic eczema for twenty years, and the skin on her face looked really ugly. Within weeks it had all gone, and she sent Dr. Wangyal a colour photo of before and after, with exuberant thanks.
>
> A friend, Josè, suffered from strong back pains. He had used painkillers and allopathic medicines for several years, even though they did not help. He had also tried different treatments without result. Then he consulted Dr. Pema Dorjee, who asked him to check his blood sugar. It was only then discovered that he suffered from diabetes. After one month on Tibetan medicines, a new blood test was taken, and the blood sugar had gone down. He happily continued with the Tibetan medicines, and his back was fine.
>
> RAGNAR had Addison's disease. After three years with Tibetan medicines, he could return to work.

Eli suffered Narcolepsy – "The Tibetan medicines helped for my general condition, though not for the fits of sleep and the paralysis which characterise this illness, I, therefore, dropped the medicines after two months. However, Dr. Wangyal was of great help. He told me that narcolepsy is not an illness, but a condition of consciousness. This explanation has taught me much about how to tackle my condition. By a daily mixture of Tai Chi, Qi Gong, Yoga and meditation I can maintain an energy level sufficient that I do not need medicines."

Maria, about seventy years old, developed calcification of the eyes. She received very light gold hammer acupuncture around the eyes with spontaneous effect.

Annie, three months old was born albino. After one month on Tibetan medicines her eye specialist noted that she had got more pigment in her eyes. Two months later, still increasing pigment. The doctor, who had thought she would not get a better sight than normal for an albino, was impressed with her face colour. The mother's comment six months later "The medicines did not taste well and it was difficult to get such a small child to take them. So I started to mix with homeopathic medicine, and after some time only used that."

Elizabeth developed some complications in menstruation. Her periods had stopped and she tried allopathic medicine. As it did not help, she tried homeopathic medicines and then ayurvedic medicines. To no avail. At last, after years, it was her regular doctor who suggested she might try Tibetan medicine. Within two months her periods were back to normal.

A polish woman who had aborted several times. After trying Tibetan medicine became pregnant, and a child was born to her.

Two Indian ladies were having difficulties in getting pregnant. After a few months' treatment both became pregnant, and delivered healthy children.

Mrs. Petersen could not get pregnant. She and her husband were checked, but the doctors found nothing wrong. She was then advised to consult a Tibetan doctor, and after one month on Tibetan medicines she became pregnant. She was very happy, and persuaded her friend Catherine to try too. After three weeks she too became pregnant. Tibetan medicine cannot help everyone, but it is certainly worth a try!

MRS. HOWE had Amoebic hepatitis. She was unable to stomach food. She suffered from diarrhoea and a sour taste in her mouth. She also suffered from numerous boils. Two months after starting with Tibetan medicines the amoebic hepatitis was cured. Then the boils disappeared, and she had no more problems.

MR. TAYLOR had haemorrhage – "I was suffering from acute bleeding. The bleeding was almost continuous. I was becoming weaker and weaker and was unable to stand. This was healed with allopathic medicine, but the doctors also wanted me to be operated on for the ulcers. Luckily I was advised by a friend to see a Tibetan doctor. I was completely cured within a month."

KENNETH had stones in the pancreas and severe damage to the pancreatic duct. He was diagnosed in two hospitals and the only solution suggested was a life saving operation. Due to severe pain he went to see Dr. Tsewang Tamdin. The pain that used to last 16-18 hours a day gradually disappeared, and was completely gone after two months.

CARMEN turned deaf, had many other problems and was unable to move. Used allopathic medicines for years with no result, and the doctors had lost all hope of her recovery. About a year after using Tibetan medicines administered by Dr. Tsewang Tamdin, she had recovered from nearly all her ailments and is able to hear clearly.

MR. BOWEN suffered epileptic fits. The allopathic doctors tried everything, but the fits not only continued, but also became more acute. He then consulted Dr. Tenzin Choedrak, and he cured the epilepsy within a few months.

MR. GOLDSTEIN who had an acute state of epilepsy, the Tibetan treatment not only cured his epilepsy, he also got back his energy. Dr. Tenzin Choedrak cured him, with no traces of epilepsy left.

MR. ANDREWS had an accident, and his epileptic fits started after a couple of years. Several renowned specialists in allopathic medicine tried to help him for years, but to little effect. After less than half a year on Tibetan medicines, administered by Dr.Tsewang Tamdin, he recovered completely.

MR. BAINES – "I had severe pain due to kidney stones, but after three weeks on Tibetan medicines, all the stone particles have passed through the urine, and I have no more pain".

MR. DOWNS suffered chronic dysentery with liver abscess. He suffered for years. And his eyes hurt too. At last he visited a Tibetan clinic, and was cured.

MRS. DAVIS suffered from chronic malaria. After three months on Tibetan medicines she recovered slowly but steadily.

MARIA NINA – "I was suffering from black patches around my mouth only. It was terrible to look at. Dr. Tsewang Tamdin cured me completely."

LYNN – "Before my exams every year, I used to have rapid palpitations and heart beat, with a pain on my left side. I used to get very nervous. But one year I had medicines prescribed by Dr. Gyurmey, and since then I have had no trouble.

The Tibetan Book: Spiritual wisdom of present and past.

Padma Basic (28)

These medicines going to Europe had a long march that started in the 19th century, via Mongolia and the south of Russia to St. Petersburg. Two brothers brought the prescription with them, lama Tsultrim Padma, and a monk, both doctors. They settled in St. Petersburg. The monk studied Western medicine and took on a Russian name. Still their Padma formula mostly consisted of Tibetan herbs, but the monk found local plants with equivalent properties and the Padma medicine became more westernised. Later, it found its way to Poland, and finally ended up in Switzerland. Here it has been manufactured for more than thirtyfive years, in accordance with the internationally recognised pharmaceutical quality guidelines.

Today Padma 28 consists of nineteen different medicinal herbs, dried and ground, but otherwise unchanged, together with natural camphor and calcium sulphate. These nineteen medicinal herbs are: Iceland moss, Castus root, Margosa fruit, Cardamom fruit, Red Sandalwood heart wood, Tropical Almond fruit, Allspice fruit, Bengal Quince fruit, Columbine aerial part, English Plantain aerial part, Liquorice root, Knotgrass aerial part, Golden Cinquefoil aerial part, Clove flower, Ginger lily rhizome, Heart leaved Sida aerial part, Valerian root, Lettuce leaf and Calendula flower. The ingredients include key natural constituents, such as polyphenols, bioflavonoids and essential oils.

The wide variety of herbs contains information beneficial to the whole spectrum of the body's defence mechanisms. As only small amounts of each individual plant are used, the supportive and healing inputs provided have a gentle effect. This medical knowledge, long applied by Tibetan doctors, has been confirmed in modern-day research laboratories in the West.

Padma 28 has a wide number of applications. It is a cooling formula, is rich in antioxidants (chemicals that protect cells from damage caused by oxidation), promotes good circulation, while the combination of ingredients reduces inflammation and supports the immune system.

Circulatory disorders:

With its many different active ingredients and protective substances, Padma 28 is effective in circulatory disorders resulting from arteriosclerosis, such as–

A. Intermittent elucidation,

B. Peripheral artery disease or

C. Peripheral vascular disease (Window viewer legs) and

D. Smokers' legs.

An investigation has been conducted in Denmark, at the clinical physiological/nuclear medical branch, Fredriksberg Hospital and at Amtsygehuset in Glostrup, its clinical chemical branch. In both investigations there were randomised double blind parallel groups set-up.

Swiss researchers carried out two equivalent investigations. In a randomised double-blind study published in the medical journal *Angiology* in 1993, 36 patients who suffered from intermittent leg pain took either a placebo or two tablets of Padma 28 twice a day. After four months the patients who took Padma 28 were able to walk twice as far as before without leg pain, while those who took the placebo showed no improvement.

Chronic respiratory tract infections:

Just as many herbs contain antioxidants and anti-inflammatory substances, they also tend to have antimicrobial activity. As the herbs in Padma 28 have all of these properties, the medicine is well suited for lung problems both in adults and children.

Several studies on chronic respiratory-tract infections and Padma 28 have been published, among them a three-year study in 2001 in Switzerland, on 305 children with chronic respiratory tract infections. They suffered at least from one infection per month over nine months, and at least three of the infections were bronchitis and/or pneumonia.

72% of the children showed a positive effect after 10 weeks' treatment with Padma 28.

Nine months after the end of the treatment, 19% showed a very good effect, 26% a good effect, and 24% a moderately good effect.

Two Polish studies concerned Padma 28 in treatment of Chronically active hepatitis type B (chronic inflammation of the liver caused by a virus). In the first, in 1992, the biochemical parameters returned to normal in 90% of the patients, and the cell-counts of the subgroups of the T-lymphocytes were improved.

In 15% the viral infection of the liver cells could be eliminated, in 70% there was a production of antibodies.

The other study, in 1993 of patients treated with Padma 28 for one year. In seventeen patients an antiviral effect was observed, which can be compared with the efficacy of interferon therapy. The anti-inflammatory effect of Padma 28 was shown by a marked improvement of biochemical parameters in 26 of the 34 patients and histology was improved in nineteen patients.

Multiple Sclerosis

In 1992 a one-year study was carried out at the neurological clinic at the Institute of Pharmacology and Toxicology, the Medical Academy in Stettin. Hundred patients suffering from MS were divided into two groups. There was no lowering of the relapse rates and a decrease in the progression of the MS in the group treated with Padma 28 and symptomatic therapies. The patients of the comparative group were only treated symptomatically. 44% of the Padma 28 trial patients showed clinical improvement, while in the comparative group no improvement was observed. On the other hand, in the comparative group who did not get Padma 28, but placebo, 40% of the patients showed deterioration, while only 12% of the group treated with Padma 28 did so.

There have also been positive effects in the treatment of Raynaud's disease, which is an illness of circular disorders in hands and feet, and in the detoxification and strengthening of the immune system.

The Massage and Herbal baths

The massage follows more or less the massage points we know from Japanese massage. The massage is never strong. Sesame oil is the most usual as massage oil. It must always be dried off after the treatment, preferably with toasted barley flour. (Toasted barley is the staple food for the Tibetans, called *Tsampa*). Because this is a time consuming treatment, this is a method the travelling Tibetan doctors do not use in the West.

Nor do they use medicinal herbal baths. Dr. Wangyal, and his assistant doctor that year, the lady doctor Sonam Lhamo, would have wished to use medicinal baths on some of the MS patients in Norway. It is a very hot deep bath with many different herbs, of which the main ingredient is juniper. This was discussed in our home. They tasted our local juniper, but were not satisfied. It was not potent enough. We had just returned from a trip to the mountains, and had some mountain juniper in the car. Tasting that, both lit up. This was excellent. But alas! the project was too complicated to carry through. They were not happy with the thought of using an ordinary bathtub with hot tap water, but normally use a bathtub on four legs, heated from below with an open fire.

The peony, a symbol of love and devotion

Cupping

Cupping is often used. In Tibet they use cups of iron, copper, silver or gold, depending on what kind of suffering the doctor will relieve. In the West they just use a drinking glass, light a piece of paper which they place under the glass held upside down, and then quickly place it over the blockage on the patient. The skin is sucked into the glass, and it turns dark red, filled with impure blood. Removing the glass, they may slit very thinly with a scalpel into the skin to release the blood. This blood is often clogged and very dark. A real blockage. In such cases the patient feels an immediate relief.

> Our friend Thubten told us he had severe pain with an aching neck after sitting bent over his studies in the Potala palace over a long period. He received cupping with a gold cup. The pain disappeared immediately and never reappeared.

> One patient had recurring headaches, due to hitting the bottom of the swimming pool with his back, when diving. It was fascinating to see how the skin that was sucked into the cupping glass, turned redder and redder. When Dr. Wangyal removed the glass, he made four cuts with his scalpel, but the blood was reluctant to appear. When it did, it was nearly black, and indeed very clogged up. The patient felt immediate relief; his head felt lighter and his back more flexible.

The rhinoceros horn is a symbol of unity.

Moxa Acupuncture

The first time I met Dr. Tenzin Choedrak in Switzerland was due to painful neck. The consultation impressed me. "Would you like to be burned?"– beamed Dr. Choedrak. I had no idea what that meant, but felt such an absolute confidence in this chap, with one eye pointing to the sky – a result of Chinese torture. Dr. Choedrak placed himself behind me, measured carefully and marked a point on the crown of my head (G20 in acupuncture), plus the upper dorsal vertebrae, and started to knead some lumps of dried Tibetan herb, leondopodium hancockii, into small cones. He placed one on the crown and another on the dorsal vertebrae, after cleansing the areas with garlic that also functioned as glue for placing the cones. Then he lit them. He started to blow on them to make them glow strongly. It really hurt! With a roaring thunderstorm outside as suitable company. The point in the neck produced a big bubble that burst and hit him in his face: "Good, good", rejoiced Dr. Choedrak, covering the burn with a little butter – and that was that. Strangely enough it did not hurt at all afterwards, and during the night I woke up feeling my troublesome neck was much better. But before that – oh dear!

Immediately after the treatment I had an audience with H.H. the Dalai Lama to interview him. God knows what I asked him about, at any rate I did not get one word down on paper. Next time I met him, I apologised, but he only laughed his deep, contagious laugh, said he was fully aware that I was by no means up to standard and why.

In Tibetan acupuncture mostly needles of silver are used, but also iron and gold. Gold is used much for psychological problems or part-problems. Western acupuncturists use silver.

Dr. Tenzin Namdul* works in the research department of Tsee-Khang, Dharamsala. The following is described by him–

---

* For details see Appendix III

Tsering has never been busier since he opened his small restaurant in one of the busy passages of Mcleodganj.[1] It was March and this is generally a period of time when all the hotels, guesthouses and restaurants are at their busiest. This is because March is a month when His Holiness the Dalai Lama bestows teaching to thousands of people flooding into this small town from all over the world.

Tsering has just finished his last order of the long day, when the dull pain he has been feeling for a while over his right shoulder, becomes sharper, but he cannot be bothered much, needing to prepare for the next hectic day. Three months after Tsering had that sharp pain, he could barely move his right shoulder. It slowly passed down to his hand and fingers, restricting any movement. Almost a year had passed, when he presented himself to a Tibetan doctor in deep frustration. The allopathic doctor had pronounced his problem as frozen shoulder and had advised anti-inflammatory pills, a painkiller and some simple exercise. After six months of Tibetan medicine treatment, he swears by its effectiveness and especially the treatment of Mey-Tsa or moxabustion that helped him get back to his normal life.

Mey-Tsa or Moxabustion is one of the accessory therapies in Tibetan medicine that involves generating heat on a specific point by burning Ta-Wa[2] (Leondopodium franchetii Beauv). Anaphalis hancockii is also used. Moxabustion helps in eliminating any disorder induced by Phlegm (Bad-kan[3])

---

[1] Mecloadganj is a small town in Dharamsala at the height of 1778 meters above sea level. It is largely inhabited by Tibetan people and is also known as 'Little Lhasa'. His Holiness the Dalai Lama has been residing here since he escaped Tibet during the Chinese invasion in 1959.

[2] *Ta-Wa* (Leontopodium franchetii Beauv) is of three types. It has a head or tip with the shape of a flower. The flower is cleaned and dried, which is then used for burning on the appropriate point in moxabustion.

[3] *Badkan (Phlegm)* is one of the three principles energies of the body manifested by earth and water elements. It is cold in nature and has characteristics of oily, cool, heavy, blunt, smooth, firm and sticky. Phlegm is responsible for firmness of the body and stability of mind. It induces sleep, connects body joints, generates tolerance and lubricates the body.

and Wind (rLoong[4]) imbalance. But it is important to understand that the moxabustion cannot be administered for every disease or every person. There are dos and don ts to follow in order to receive the maximum benefit and avoid any complications.

How to administer:

It can be administered generally on any disorder caused by Phlegm and Wind imbalance leading to weak metabolic heat, indigestion, dropsy, *cold* Bile (Tripa[5]) disorder, muscular and bone tumour, muscular spasm, empty fever, i.e., a fever which is influenced by Wind, where the patient has a sensation of fever even though the temperature doesn't go up, and even for psychiatric problems, forgetfulness and any neural disorder.

It should not be administered for any diseases induced by hot and blood disorder. It should also be avoided on the points of the five sense organs (eyes, nose, mouth, ears and tongue), genital organ and six hollow organs (gall bladder, stomach, large and small intestine, urinary bladder and reproductive organ) straight after eating any food. This treatment is not to be used for pregnant women, or for obese people.

There are a few guidelines the patient has to follow after the treatment of moxabustion: the patient has to take a few steps right after being treated with the moxabustion; he/she also has to make sure to keep away from cold and not to expose himself/herself to water. No shower, no bath.

---

[4] *rLoong (Wind)* is one of the three principles energies of the body manifested by the air element. It is characterized as rough, light, cold, subtle, hard and mobile. Wind acts as a medium between mind and body. It maintains the function of physical and mental activities; any movement in the body like, respiration, urination, defecation, development and delivery of the foetus, menstruation, spitting, burping, speech, etc, and clarity of the sense organs.

[5] *Tripa (Bile)* is one of the three principle energies of the body manifested by the fire element. It is hot in nature and is characterized by oily, sharp, hot, light, fetid, purgative and fluid. Bile is responsible for hunger, thirst, digestion and assimilation, promotes bodily heats, gives clarity to body complexion, and provides courage and determination.

Movement after the treatment is important, Dr. Lobsang Wangyal explained it in this way – "After a moxabustion you should dance, after bloodletting you should sleep".

When employing moxabustion, it is also important to consider the calculation of Tibetan astrology. The physician has to find the right time and day in accordance with the patient's date of birth. It is not advisable to administer the treatment on the day of the full moon.

> MR. LANCET had a chronic indigestion problem. Slightly heavy or improper food gave him sharp pain and flatulence. He tried different medicines without any success. Eventually he took to Tibetan medicine and got effectively treated by a combination of medicine and moxabustion. The moxabustion was administered to revive the metabolic heat.

In Tibetan medicine, accompanying therapy is employed only when other modalities of treatment like diet, behaviour and medicine do not work, or do not prove that effective.

While doing moxabustion, it is very important to identify the appropriate point for particular ailments. There are certain points, which the physician can identify from the disease or pain itself. When we press the particular point where the patient is complaining of pain/discomfort, the patient will feel relaxed and the particular site will sink a bit. Other than that, someone having pulled a nerve due to causes such as a sharp twist, or lifting heavy things, can also be brought into this category.

The important points, which the physician has to trace, are the internal organs. There are 71 different points in total to administer the moxabustion. The Ta-Wa has to be prepared to a specific size depending on the location and sensitivity of the point. It is made into a cone, placed on the point using garlic juice as a glue and disinfectant, and then lit. The doctor blows on the glowing cone to increase the heat. Definitely painful, but it lasts only for a minute or so, and even though the treatment leaves a third degree burn, it does not hurt any more.

The wound now oozes matter for a couple of weeks, and should not be treated, and only covered with a light bandage, allowing the wound to "breathe". Some feel an immediate relief, others an increasing relief during the following days.

However, gentle moxabustion may also be given, depending on the illness, by generating heat at the particular point by placing the burning herb near the surface of the skin, but not literally touching it. In instances using vital points such as main nerves or sensitive areas like the face or close to the eyes, the burning can be discarded before it reaches or touches the skin.

> An old woman in a small village in Nepal had a minor stroke along with a chronic arthritis problem. The disease left an impact on her right shoulder and hand, making it stiff. Over the years, the fingers of the right hand had become numb and folded, with total loss of grip. The Tibetan physician did a moxabustion on five different points on her hand, and her fingers slowly unfolded out at that very moment, making her a very happy person. She couldn't control her feelings exclaiming, "I simply can't believe it". After a few sessions of therapy along with Tibetan medicine, her hand and fingers rediscovered the pleasure of movement.

The Tibetan Book: Spiritual wisdom of present and past.

Gold Hammer Acupuncture

All the accessory therapies like golden needle therapy, gold hammer therapy, cupping, venesection, hydrotherapy, massage, etc., date back some 3000 years.

The gold hammer is an instrument with a tip of pure gold. It is heated and then applied on the wanted spots. This gives a second-degree burn. It hurts too, but that only lasts seconds. This type of treatment may improve blood circulation, reduce high blood pressure, improve the digestive heat, heal wounds and swellings, ease pain, especially when it concerns shoulder pain, arthritis and rheumatism, reduces the synovial fluid in the joints, helps diseases related to the nervous system, like Multiple Sclerosis, Parkinson's disease and spondylitis, and may ease mental problems, when, e.g., used on the acupuncture point G20.

These therapies are very effective but it is important to know when you have to administer this particular therapy and for what particular constitution it is suitable.

After an interview with Dr. Lobsang Wangyal on the radio in Norway, we received a letter. An elderly lady who believed in it explained this method to me. Old Norwegian medicine has a similar method to the moxabustion, which has probably been forgotten today. It was called – "To burn tinder against gout". A little ball, from a fungus growing on birch trees, was kneaded, dipped in turpentine or paraffin, placed on the painful spot – in the elderly lady's case it was sciatica – and lit. A blister formed, it burst, and the higher the ball went into the air, the better: That is the "gout-wind" disappearing. Painful – yes, of course".

This letter came from the North of Norway, and I guess it may have shamanistic roots. When H.H. Dalai Lama visited the Lapps in the North in the year when he received the Nobel Peace Prize, he recognized a special little drum exactly like the one used in Tibetan ceremonies. Perhaps there had been a communication in olden times? It is after all well known, that old tales have wandered to and from Eastern countries along a Northern route.

Some case histories:

> ROY: "After the car accident I suffered from headaches, muscle aches, nervousness and depression. After fifteen days treatment, with moxa, gold hammer, massage and medicines, I am perfectly all right."
>
> TROND, 51 years: Trapped nerves in the back. According to the Tibetan doctor the cause was lifting too heavy objects, and not dressing warmly enough – which increases Wind.

Received gold hammer acupuncture early in 1991, and was symptom free for six-seven years. Periodically got worse, and received another moxa treatment on two acupuncture points in 2000.

KAREN had hyper mobile spine. Stable after one treatment, but was careless and lifted too heavy too early – a typical Wind reaction.

MR. WILCOX: Was suffering from spondylosis, the nervous system did not function well, his neck was stiff, which resulted in sudden fits of giddiness to such an extent that he was unable to work. He was greatly helped by Tibetan moxabustion, and the precious pill moon crystal.

RUTH had unstable pelvis and false milk production, hair loss. Had never been pregnant. Arrived on crutches, received moxa acupuncture and threw the crutches away the same day. The milk production and loss of hair stopped.

The lozenge is a symbol of victory.

Hormay Therapy

Hormay therapy is a very mild type of treatment. This is a heat treatment on acupuncture points for Wind energy, and is *only* used for Wind problems of cold nature, such as dizziness, fainting, heart palpitations, insomnia, ringing in the ear, stiff limbs and many other Wind disturbances. However, many of these symptoms may have other characteristics, and it is strongly warned against using Hormay therapy for hot diseases, and where the main problems are based on Bile and Blood.

Cumin seeds (or caraway seeds) are crushed and wrapped in thin gauze to a firm and closely tied little ball. The ball is dipped in heated mustard oil or sesame oil, and lightly pressed toward the specific Wind points.

Here are some case histories concerning Goldhammer and moxa acupuncture to awaken your curiosity:

> ARNOLD, 37 years old suffered from constant pains due to a totally worn down vertebrae (L4). So worn it could hardly be discerned on the X-ray. The doctors did not dare to operate. He was doubled with pain when he arrived. After the treatment with the deep moxa acupuncture on two spots, he was told to walk around the room. The pain had already vanished! The Tibetan doctors say that after moxa acupuncture you should dance, after bloodletting you should not budge, so that little walk was part of the treatment. When Arnold had a new X-ray taken a year later, the vertebrae had regenerated. Incredible!
>
> Scott, 50 years old had spinal problems. Severe pain, wore a corset for eight months, and had to sit in a chair to sleep. The Western doctors said the chance that an operation would help, was 50-50. In 1993 he came to see the Tibetan doctor, and got deep moxa on five acupuncture points on his back. He felt how the pain ran out through his legs during the treatment, and was totally without pain for six years.

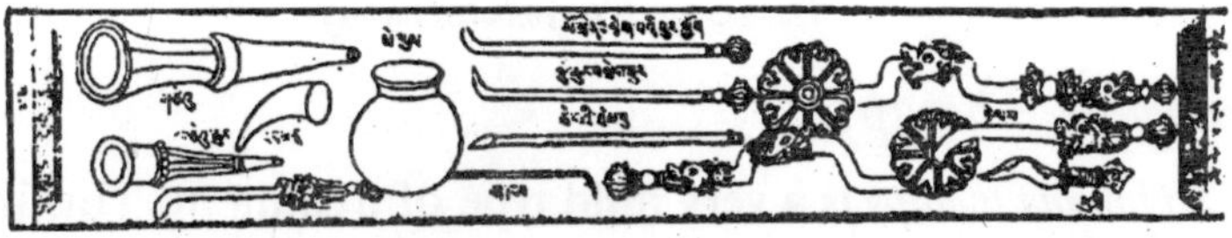

Instruments used in Tibetan medicine for acupuncture, cupping and bloodletting.

[6] *Gyud-shi* (Four Tantra) is the fundamental text of Tibetan medicine. It was first written by Elder Yuthok Yonten Gonpo in eighth century and later revised by Younger Yuthok Y. Gonpo in twelfth century. Moxabustion is fully described here.

We are at war with nature, and should we by chance win this war, we are the losers.

E.F. Schumacher
author of the book *Small is Beautiful.*

The flaming jewel is an old Buddhist symbol.
It can contain six or three jewels. If there are three, these symbolise Buddha (teacher). Dharma (the teaching) and Sangha (the community)

Chapter - VI

TREATEMENT OF SPECIFIC ILLNESS

The Tibetan doctor determines the treatment by changing the diet and/or lifestyle according to the pattern of problems in the patients:

Cold,
Warm,
Cold + warm,
Wind,
Bile,
Phlegm,
Blood and their combinations.

Diet and behaviour are vital concerning chronic illnesses, and are often complicated to decipher. Remember that it can be complicated, when you try to regulate the diet by yourself, as you might do after studying which temperament you think you are, and the Yes and No tables (See p. 40).

Very often we find a combined illness, where the patient should have the opposite diet to what he uses. It can be quite a puzzle to find out what one can tolerate and what not.

> A person was fat and heavy, and could blow into a rage. He was mad on chocolate and cakes. The man had suffered a head injury some years ago, and concentrated sweets can

> have a trigger effect for brain damage. It took the doctor some time to convince him that the chocolate and cakes triggered his anger. He agreed to give the doctor's advice a chance. Within weeks his rage had gone. But he missed the cakes and chocolates, and had another go. Again he exploded with anger. That gave him the necessary proof.
>
> Another persons in his sixties had strong asthma. He could not even cross the street without using his inhaler. About once a month he was rushed to hospital in an ambulance. What did he fancy? Two litres of milk daily! Milk creates phlegm, and Phlegm creates imbalance, and is specifically detrimental to asthma patients. Our patient was told to quit milk, but he reacted as if he were an alcoholic: "Oh no, that could not be the cause". The asthma got worse, so after another six months he agreed to try quitting the milk. A few months later our asthma patient was cured. No medicines were given. The best proof of his cure was that he himself put new grass turf on the roof of his cottage.
>
> A married couple were told by the Tibetan doctor to change their diets. The husband had a hot disease and the wife a cold disease. They had some problem sorting *that* out in their daily diet! But they did, and were rewarded with a cure, with their opposing individual diets. As the old saying goes "One man's meat is another man's poison".

If you have a chronic disease, try if you can decipher the following yourself: Do you have a hot or a cold disease? If it is cold, you easily shiver with cold, have cold hands or feet, have shifting pains, lack of energy and heaviness of body. What food do you like specifically, even if you do not have a special craving? The answer may be rewardingly obvious!

However, when you think you have a cold disease, Wind or Phlegm, or Wind + Phlegm combined, and Bile could also be part of the picture. If the Wind is hot, than you have actually a combined cold/hot disease involving Bile. So it may be very difficult to try being your own doctor, after all. Professional help is highly recommended! Many acupuncturists may for instance give some advice regarding the diet based on the principles of cold and warm – Yin and

Yang, Ayurvedic therapists even more so. In many cases it can suffice to change diet, lifestyle and environment.

According to Tibetan medicine cucumber can be specifically harmful in arthritis, being sweet and cold, of the Water element. Arthritis in itself is a cold disease, of the Water element.

If the person with his chronic illness tries to drop the "drug", be it alcohol or milk or chocolate, he actually craves more, because he gets withdrawal symptoms. He misinterprets that, and thinks it is what he needs!

It is really quite usual for people with a craving to reject the view that the specific craving could be the cause of the illness. It is certainly not only alcoholics who will not accept where their problems lie!

I wonder how many patients of Western doctors get medicines and go through an operation "unnecessarily", instead of changing their diet? Because their problem is really caused by having developed a chronic disease due to false indulgences?

Further step of treatment is the medication.

The raw materials for the medicines are mainly herbs and minerals, with some animal ingredients in some medicines, but there are no active toxic or narcotic stimulant elements in them.

There are always several ingredients in one pill. If there is any toxic substance in it, this is detoxified. Once, the Health Authorities contacted us because a medicine contained *nux vomica*, which is poisonous, and thus not allowed. However, the poisonous nux vomica is boiled in milk, and this detoxifies the poison. So some ingredients in the pill may not be for the illness itself, but to harmonise the ingredients.

Another medicine contains mercury, but this is processed in a very special way, through a highly complicated process lasting more than three months, with close observation continually day and night. Highly trained doctors do the process, as a mere negligence could lead to hazardous health problems. This medicine had to be dropped in Norway at the time, as it was too difficult to explain to the health authorities how it had been detoxified.

I got it myself from Dr. Wangyal during a visit to India. When I went for a medical check to my ordinary doctor in Norway on return, he was alarmed by the high contents of mercury in the blood, "on the verge of having to go to hospital". I tried to tell him that this was actually very favourable, as the mercury was being transported out of the body through the blood. My somewhat sceptical doctor asked me to undergo a new blood test two weeks later, and then the mercury had nearly disappeared in the blood. The doctor was surprised as well as reassured.

To make it clear, it is not possible to buy Tibetan medicines in the open market. Tibetan medicines can only be prescribed by a consulting Tibetan doctor. However, one medicine available is *Padma 28 (PadmaBasic* in the US). This medicine, produced in Switzerland, has helped many.

The vase contains spiritual jewels.

High Blood Pressure

In Tibetan medicine we say that the blood presses towards the walls of the arteries. This can be a disturbance in Pervasive Wind, which resides in the heart and operates throughout the whole circulatory system. Another cause is too much or too thick blood in the vessels, which causes pressure on its flow.

One of the most important functions of Wind energy is to open and close all the pathways, which includes the heart.

Unhealthy food and wrong lifestyle disturbs this specific Wind energy.

High blood pressure due to *Wind disturbance* is found among people who are weak, anaemic, depressed, suffering from multiple childbirth, old age, post-surgery, traumatized childhood, or after prolonged illness as well as a Wind temperament. This may be caused by fasting, lack of sleep, cold wind, tragedy, stress and tension, persistent noise, extreme cold, wet and/or windy climate.

It is also caused by over consumption of coffee and tea, which is light and rough in nature. It catapults the pressure of the Wind in the bloodstream and propels it to the upper extremities of the body. Rancid food, cold and dry food is also harmful. Salt should be avoided completely.

Not attending to the call of nature, and holding back all the natural impulses (wind, sneezing, belching), can also lead to high blood pressure. Too little and too intense exercise is another factor.

Avoid all food with coarse and light potencies, which can increase the Wind energy, such as coffee, tea, ice cream, cold water, lemon, sugar, green vegetables, bitter gourd, capsicum, white flour, white rice, dry biscuits and schwann pepper.

Fresh food and fresh meat and vegetable fat, especially sesame oil, and also onion and garlic soups can be beneficial. Resting in bed and pleasant words from close friends also help.

> Mr. Dale aged 64 had increased blood pressure, blood sugar, and formation of gas in the abdomen. He was suffering from gout. He tried allopathic as well as homeopathic medicine. When first taking the Tibetan medicines from Dr. Tenzin Norbu, the first reactions was increased pain from the gout, coughs and a congested throat, but gradually the symptoms disappeared. After six months the blood pressure became stable, so was the blood sugar, as well as his general health. This case included Wind as well as Phlegm.

High blood pressure of the *Bile type* can be caused by long exposure to the sun's heat, extreme and tedious physical labour, mental and physical disturbance, which results in restlessness of body, of speech and of mind, and over consumption of alcohol, fats, spices and too much nutritious food. This increases the heat of the body, which speeds up blood circulation and thus results in high blood pressure.

Avoid hot, salty and sour food, spicy food (hot!), too much nettle, spinach and animal fat.

> BRUCE suffered from high blood pressure for years. He used allopathic medicines, but the side effects made more medicines necessary, again giving more side effects. He was constantly tired, and his focus was suffering too. This did not go well with his job, where he needed to be very dynamic. The Tibetan doctor advised him on his diet, and convinced him that he must do something with his job situation. Fed up as Bruce was, he was willing to try "even that", and after a few months he was quite a different person. He had got his energy back, and his concentration too.

There is no specific classification of high blood pressure due to *Phlegm*, but usually it is considered that obesity, a sedentary lifestyle, rich food and lack of physical exercise are some of the factors. Alcohol and coffee should be avoided totally. Weight must be brought down. Weak uncoloured tea is O.K. Fruit and fruit juices, curd and skimmed milk are favourable. Bitter pumpkin, cauliflower and green leaf vegetables are also recommended.

> MRS. WILSON had a problem of faulty breath amounting to choking sensations for the last twenty years or so. No allopathic treatment had been of any use. After about a month of treatment from Dr. Tenzin Choedrak, she recovered remarkably and is now fully cured. The problem of high blood pressure is also under control.

Here is an opposite reaction:

> MR. BARKER had very dry skin, loss of sleep, low blood pressure, never got enough sleep and suffered from extreme weakness. His skin problem disappeared totally after a year

and a half, and his sleep was back to normal, after starting with Tibetan medicines. The blood problem has improved, and he can work much more.

Chrysanthemum: The flower of autumn.

Arthrosis/Arthritis

This is a condition usually caused by essential nutrients not being absorbed. This causes body fluids to increase. It can be made worse by oily and calorie rich food, and by staying in wet and damp places.

The different types are pale, mixed and dark arthritis. The symptoms are similar in all three types, but what triggers the illness differs.

Pale or Phlegm arthritis: The digestion is too slow. This results in increased Phlegm. The patient loses energy, feels mentally heavy and tired. Sleeps too much, especially during the day after meals containing a lot of fat. This may in addition develop into asthma if the patient stays in humid and cold areas.

The skin colour becomes pale, and the patient feels inwardly cold. The increased phlegm then spreads to the limbs. There are five types of Phlegm, which have special function in the body (as shown in the article on Phlegm, page 20). One of them is called the Phlegm connection between the limbs, same as mixing or decomposing Phlegm. This influences the limbs as well as the connection between the limbs. It is a cold disease.

Mixed or Wind arthritis: This is caused by stress and an irregular lifestyle, such as skipping meals and not getting enough sleep. Cold is its worst enemy. This again is a cold disease.

Dark or Bile (blood) arthritis: It starts with fever, and may be caused by a previous illness where the patient has not taken the fever seriously, left the bed before the fever had gone, and gone back to work. Or been exposed to physical or mental stress during the period of fever. With that the fever does not leave the body, but becomes chronic and sinks into the joints. The patient may also have started to eat fatty food, meat and been drinking alcohol before the fever left the body. This is a hot disease.

It is difficult to choose the correct medicine. There are many that help against arthritis, and many elements from the diagnosis have to be considered. The correct choice gives very good results. Then Pale arthritis may be cured within a year, Mixed arthritis in two years, and Dark arthritis in three years.

With Pale and Mixed arthritis the patient should have a warm herbal bath in spring and another in autumn, followed by a massage with walnut oil. Its purpose is to make the patient sweat profusely. After one year moxa acupuncture along the spine is given for Pale arthritis, and after two years for Mixed arthritis. With Dark arthritis the choice of medicines is even more important.

The patient in addition receives a herbal bath, the second spring, but without massage. After this bath the Dark arthritis will flare strongly, and the patient gets a liquid medicine to separate the bad from the healthy blood. A few days later blood is let from a special point on the inside of the ankle – it is then dark and black. As soon as the blood shows a healthy colour, the blood letting is stopped. If the patient also has high blood pressure, this treatment may have to be repeated the next autumn.

A patient with dark arthritis must stick to a fairly strict diet, and refrain from alcohol, meat and sweet food. All arthritis patients should avoid raw cucumbers, and often potatoes, especially if they are cooked and served cold. Cold milk is not recommended – it should be boiled. The worst is cold milk in hot tea. (I suppose that is why the English always use hot milk in their tea). Freshly boiled water on a fasting heart is excellent, and may be taken for five days before starting with the medicines.

Usually an arthritic patient is worse in the morning. Then it is important to be active, to recover quicker.

The treatment should consist of a change in diet, of exercise, medicines that improve the metabolism and circulation, and acupuncture treatment on the spine.

The arthritis can be of a cold or a hot type:

Hot arthritis together with serious infections, is caused by oily and calorie rich food, and curd, pickles and pepper may cause infection in the synovial fluid. It can also be caused by contagious fever, and mechanical injuries.

Cold arthritis, where there are no serious infections, is due to prolonged stays in damp places, and too many cold baths or due to obesity and a sedentary lifestyle. It can also become worse by food we are not used to, and by food that is heavy to digest. One should avoid oily and salty food. Avoid sour, cold and fried food and also rancid and heavy food. Favourable food is barley, beans, and buttermilk, boiled lukewarm water, weak uncoloured tea and other items, which have a warm and light character. Porridge and other barley flour dishes are highly recommended.

A controlled fasting using light fibre food is also favourable, as it cleanses the blood. Avoid sleeping in the daytime. Limit physical activities, walk evenly with pauses, do not walk quickly for too long. Fasting, rest and mild exercise is essential for the treatment of arthritis. Massage helps in some cases, as it stimulates the flow of blood through the joints and thereby reduces pain.

Primary cause: The lymphatic system and the excretions do not function well due to deficient digestion and wrong life style. It can also be Karmic.

Lotus — the flower of summer. Stands for absolute purity.

Rheumatism

Causes: Living in wet or damp areas. Excessive use of food items that are oily or very nutritious, and do not get assimilated easily. Then the morbid substances are transformed into lymph fluid. This is collected in the body and scattered in flesh, bone, lymphatic system and ligaments by the Wind. This results in rheumatism affecting the muscles, the bone, the blood vessels, the ligaments and tendons. Rheumatism is affected by Wind and Phlegm, Blood and Bile.

Rheumatic arthritis is divided into six types:

Muscular, bone, nerves, lymph vessels, white arthritis and black arthritis.

General symptoms for rheumatism in *muscles* are, shivering and chilliness, irritations in skin and flesh, oily face, pain in head, waist and hips, fatigue, lethargy, loss of weight, sweating profusely, burning sensation in bones, joints and flesh, stiff ligaments, pain when moving, The colour of the urine will be red and the pulse thin.

Special symptoms, where rheumatism in the muscles phlegm and bile dominate. There is swelling in the muscles, with a dark colour, discomfort in lungs and heart, bleeding nose, a sensation as if flesh and bones separate.

Rheumatism in the *bones* is dominated by Wind problems. The symptoms are thirst, increasing heat in the bone structure. The bones become thin and the disturbance spreads to the joints. In great pain, the patient is reluctant to move. He feels as if he has been thrown from a high place, if someone moves his body or if he is exposed to high sounds.

Rheumatism in the *bloodstream* is dominated by Blood disturbances. There is discomfort in heart and lungs, it feels as if the hip muscles are falling down, the veins stand out and are hard and painful.

Rheumatism in the *ligaments.* Tendons and ligaments become stiff and hard, they are bent and become dry.

White rheumatism is due to the white lymph, which generally is of a cold nature, while *black* rheumatism is due to the dark lymph, which generally is of a warm nature.

Treatment: During the first five days it is necessary to purify the lymph with a decoction. The patient should drink boiled hot water frequently, and medicines which will dry up lymph. From time to time it will be good to induce sweat. It is also effective if a patient can visit a natural hot spring. My experience is that Tibetan medicine is especially effective for rheumatism.

As specific treatment, a mixture of musk, saffron and ginger together with curd is favourable if the illness is of a *hot* character. If the illness is *cold,* we make it with a syrup and donkey blood. Well, that is in India! Then follows a medicine that will wash out the system. With swelling of the muscles, contraction of the ligaments and pains in the legs, the patient would benefit from a medicinal bath. Afterwards the body is massaged with a mixture of medicinal butter and medical herbs. Accumulation of fluid in the joints is drawn out with a "cold spoon therapy" – a very cold spoon is applied to specific points.

The diet should include rice, coarse grain, porridge of toasted grain, chickpeas, curd with dandelion and whey, boiled cooled water and tea. This indicates that the diet should have a cooling and light potency. Avoid cured, marinated and sour food, fat, heavy food, and salt.

Regarding lifestyle and behaviour, the patient should avoid damp areas, air-conditioned rooms and fans. It is advisable to undertake regular exercise and massage. Medicinal baths with specific Tibetan herbs are also effective.

The Sorig massage oil prepared by Men-Tsee-Khang is very effective for those who have problems with ligaments, nerves and muscles in this ailment. It is of paramount importance for the patient to stay away from mental stress and tension, with proper care from those around him.

Avoid excessive heat, humidity and cold, and sleeping during the daytime. If the fever symptoms have disappeared after the above treatment, the remains of impure lymph and fever are dried up with medicinal butter with honey, beer and bovine broth. When the fever symptoms are gone, the patient can take easy walks in dry surroundings.

ARNY, 11 years: Young Arny who suffered from Arthritis was somewhat crippled, and had to use crutches. Three years later under continued Tibetan medications the crutches had gone! He cycles and plays football. His Norwegian doctors cannot understand how this could happen.

SHEILA had vasculitis and arthritis. After years on allopathic medicines with no cure, she tried Tibetan medicines and was almost completely cured within one month of treatment.

BELLE, 51 years old, suffered from spinal rheumatism (Morbus Bechterew). This is how she herself describes her situation: "Repetitive infections in the air tract, and other infections, as a child. Rheumatic symptoms started in 1976, with increasing stiffness in the back and pains/inflammations in the knees. I turned vegetarian in 1980 that helped quite a bit. The diagnosis Morbus Bechterew was given in 1981. By now I had lasting problems with back, knees and hips – was on crutches for nearly a year. Then I tried a 4 weeks' stay at a health resort in Germany, plus several alternative treatments: Antroposophic medicine, acupuncture etc. I started to eat fish in addition to the vegetarian diet; that helped generally, though only to a certain degree. I still had problems, especially with the back. From 1990 onwards, treatment once a year from Dr. Lobsang Wangyal and his successors – with moxa and gold hammer acupuncture and herbal medicines. The recommended diet and new instructions regarding my lifestyle (Wind + Phlegm = cold disease) seemed to reduce the rheumatism to a milder form. The positive effect of Moxa on the back pains was quite extraordinary. The back had not been so free, strong and without pain or stiffness in years, as during the first year after this treatment. At the consultation the following year, Dr. Wangyal said it was not necessary to use deep moxa. Gold hammer acupuncture sufficed.

What has also made a lasting impression from the Tibetan doctors' treatment is their ability to give an exact diagnosis. In addition to their insight in how diet and lifestyle can affect health and well-being. When I am nervous or depressed, I often try to meditate and get into the atmosphere the doctors create, in that way to receive more energy, power and calm with which to meet daily life. It would bring better quality to the lives of busy and stressed Norwegians, if more had the opportunity to meet the Tibetan doctors."

ANETTE had rheumatoid arthritis, after-effects of sexual abuse, hormone imbalance, and previous anorexia. "I tried several alternative medicines, one was laser therapy for years, and in the end I came to a point where I needed long-term treatment for mental problems. I found the medical knowledge on this point lacking, and my regular doctor supported me in my choices within alternative medicine. When I first came to the Tibetan doctor in 1994, I had an acute hormone imbalance. I menstruated three times per month, with only a few hours respite before it started all over again. After only two weeks on Tibetan medicine, my hormone balance was restored. After about six months I had a queer feeling in my body: I felt hunger! Since a tough anorexia in 1989, I had not felt that."

Two books together: A sign of good augury.

Stomach Ulcer

This can appear in the stomach, the duodenum and other parts of the digestive tract, and is called Brown Phlegm, which is a combined imbalance of Wind, Bile, Phlegm and Blood. Its seat is in the stomach, liver, large and small intestines, and also covers illnesses other than stomach ulcer. (The expression Brown Phlegm is used to illustrate the colour combination of the illness. Wind is blue, Bile is yellow, Phlegm is white and Blood is red.) Being an amalgamation of all the humours, it takes a long time to cure. This particular ailment has a strong connection to state of mind. The less you are exposed to stress, the better.

Hot type stomach ulcer becomes worse with sour and hot food. Oily food and fatiguing activities should be avoided. Do not keep the stomach empty for a long time. Fresh fish and beef, pulses, light food and boiled lukewarm water are recommended.

Cold type stomach ulcer is aggravated by loss of digestive heat. Avoid heavy, food which is hard to digest, fresh flour, sausages, oil, frozen food, garlic, curd and oily food. Avoid sleeping during the daytime, and avoid cold environments. Avoid nervous stress, irregular meals, tobacco and alcohol. Get enough sleep, and small but frequent regular meals.

Fresh water fish, fresh mutton, and bread, etc., with barley flour is favourable. A brisk walk is good.

The lotus: A symbol of purity

Constipation

According to Tibetan medicine this is due to wrong diet, wrong lifestyle and detrimental influences that disturb the normal function of the three temperaments. Constipation has increased with civilisation, increased competition and industrialism. In primitive societies you obey the functions of the body when they appear, instead of waiting till it "suits you". Stress as well as immobility influences the whole muscular system.

A well-known cause is lack of liquid and too much refined food, such as white flour and white sugar. This does not give the stomach enough fibre to stimulate the intestines to function, and therefore undermines the vitality of the whole system. Constipation can also be due to milk products, flour cooked with milk, dried meat and some fruits, like banana. Constant overeating also causes it, because it disturbs the function of the body energies.

The constipation may often be combined with many illnesses, like acute fever, stomach ulcers, liver and bile diseases, hysteria, anaemia and diverse chronic diseases.

Tibetan medicine thinks that most cancers start with indigestion. If one has another illness in addition to constipation, it is probable that the cause of that illness will disappear when the constipation is cured. Because with prolonged constipation, the morbid substances go into the bloodstream and will lead to toxins in the body and possibly skin diseases as well.

For some it is enough to use coarse-grained instead of white flour. If your natural digestive heat is sharp, fresh ripe fruit and salads plus dried fruits, it can help, because they are the best resources of energy due to their natural content of sugar. However, as natural digestive heat is by nature Phlegm, normally one should use such fruits and salads sparingly.

To avoid constipation meals should be regular at fixed hours. Avoid irritating, spicy and fatty food. When using fruit juices, boiled or raw vegetables, it is advisable to combine them with light meals.

Water is an excellent dissolvent. Drink as much water as possible, preferably freshly boiled, especially if you suffer from a cold disease.

Strong tea and coffee should definitely be avoided! Emotional stress and influences also give signals to the digestion, so try to avoid them, especially at mealtimes. No quarrels at the dinner table!

In short, exercise daily, eat light meals at regular hours, and drink boiled water daily to avoid constipation.

The chrysanthemum – a symbol of autumn, and of joviality.

Asthma

Traditional Tibetan medicine thinks that the causes of this type of asthma are digestive problems, obesity and phlegm.

Asthma is called UK-SAK in Tibetan: UK means "breath", and SAK means "accumulation". In Tibetan medicine accumulation of food particles that are not absorbed, is considered a main cause, because this increases the surplus of mucus. Continuous surplus of mucus influences the breathing organs and prevents the passage of air.

What causes asthma?

Overindulgent eating of cold and raw food, drinks such as cold milk and yoghurt, citrus fruits and fermented products, increase the production of mucus. If such food is eaten regularly without the body getting enough time to digest it, this will induce asthma, because the accumulation of liquid in the body, as mucus reduces the resistance of the body to all kinds of allergens.

Weakening in the organs can develop into asthma because of unhealthy combinations in the diet, or an unhealthy lifestyle, such as too little exercise. Persons of the Phlegm or Wind types are especially susceptible to these allergens (Asthma is a cold disease). Some of the most usual allergens are chemicals, house dust, fungus, pollen, cats and dogs. Such attacks do not necessarily indicate asthma at the outset. Under constant influence however, one will in time develop asthma. Poor function in some of the vital organs may also cause allergic asthma.

One of the main causes of modern asthma is pollution, especially in the bigger cities. The residues of industry influence us all, through exhaust and tobacco smoke. Escape of poisonous gases, such as carbon monoxide, nitrogen oxide and carbonic hydrogen oxide cause diverse allergic reactions such as irritated eyes and skin, worsening of asthma attacks, chronic bronchitis, and lung cancer and heart problems.

Many asthmatics complain about digestive problems, this is part of the picture of asthma and must be treated together with the asthma. According to Tibetan medicine, it is digestive Bile, decomposing Phlegm and fire like Wind, which are responsible for digestion and assimilation of the food particles. They are also responsible for maintaining a good balance of other parts of the physical constituents in the body.

Among these principles, Phlegm first breaks down the food to simpler substances, Bile produces heat to further the process of digestion, and at last Wind helps to pick up the nutrients.

Remember not to fill more than three quarters of the stomach. The fourth part is necessary to give room for the digestive job. Loss of body heat, which is necessary to digest and acquire the nourishment, causes a poor collection, which leads to an increased accumulation of mucus in the digestive system. The food particles therefore become poisonous in the digestive system. If Bile is too weak, the residues will influence fluid to be retained, and that in its turn produces mucus. The mucus settles in the bronchia, lungs and brain, and also the lymph system, sinuses and in other organs. The weak digestive heat therefore gives a poorer assimilation of the food.

The asthma attacks are made worse by colds, because mucus then leaks to the bronchia, and layers of collected mucus after repeated colds thicken and block the air passages. The breath becomes laboured and hinders the normal flow of air to the lungs. Loss of heat and a reduced regulatory system in the organs can lead to loss of resistance energy in that organ.

Tibetan medicine divides asthma into five types:

Mild: Light fits due to over-exertion in work or exercise, after having eaten a heavy meal, or staying put for a long period.

Dark: Accumulation of mucus causes blockages in the bronchia. The patient can produce too much sputum, with hoarseness, discomfort during sleep, and shooting pains in the upper part of the back. The patient may feel surrounded by darkness – thus the name.

Out breath: Breathing out is hampered by a weakened upward movement of air, due to accumulation of mucus in the bronchia. The patient has a low and short tone of voice.

In breath: The patient has no difficulties in exhalation. The inhaling is hampered because the passage of air is blocked by too much accumulation of mucus.

Strong: Hoarseness, dry throat, high-pitched tone of voice. The patient produces much sputum and finds it difficult to breathe when he starts to move. This is a serious type of asthmatic attack.

How to avoid asthma ?

The treatment is of course dependent on the cause of the asthma. Tibetan medicines and inhalation therapy often ease the acute attacks. In Tibetan medicine many factors are considered for the treatment, such as age, personal type, physical strength as well as the psychical, in addition to Wind, Phlegm, the digestive system and the other asthma factors according to the categories mentioned above. The medicines given are often progressive. The patients start with three different medicines, which are changed as development occurs, and can end up with twenty different medicines in all, which partly relieve each other.

Besides the medicines, it is necessary to regulate diet, exercise and lifestyle. One should for instance avoid exposing oneself to extremely hot or extremely cold environments, too extreme changes between cold and hot, as a cold shower after a hot sports activity (this may be one of the causes of so many top sportsmen developing asthma), sitting in strong sunshine and then taking a cold swim, moving from an air-conditioned room to extreme heat and the reverse. Normally one can tolerate some abrupt changes, but at times the body will not tolerate that.

Regular exercise, such as walking, cycling, swimming, plus breathing exercises, will strengthen and increase the lung capacity, strengthen the heart and the digestive system, because it increases the digestive heat. But strenuous and stressful exercise should be avoided.

A balanced diet is also important, as the digestive heat is weak. Warm food and warming spices are important, and garlic and ginger is recommended. Do not drink anything cold. Warm drinks with the food lower the production of mucus, and increase the digestive heat.

However, if the patient has sinus problems, he should be cautious with garlic, spinach, cucumber, carrots, onions and sweet food. When they are used, they should be boiled. Raw food is not favourable for asthma.

Avoid alcohol and smoking, fried and spicy food. You may drink colourless tea, and weak coffee sparingly. Fresh butter, warm milk plus fish, is recommended. Goat's milk can be good for asthma and breathing problems. Daily use of boiled warm water also helps to cleanse the mucus.

Avoid humid and cold environments. Moderate exercise is good.

BRIDGET was only fifteen, with a stubborn bronchial asthma. The allopathic doctors who treated her, strangely enough did not discover that she had been drinking milk "all day" since she was eight. Of course the continued consumption of milk worked against all the medicines she took. The medicines "softened" the symptoms, but the asthma was persistent. The Tibetan doctor told her to drop milk, and gave her medicines for three months. Then she was cured. Milk increases phlegm.

Ten year-old BOBBY lived in a fishing village, and just the smell of the catch and the fishing boats made him react. He only took the medicines for a few months, because his parents immediately grasped the point that they had to move from the village. They moved inland, away from the sea air they had believed to be so healthy. For a while, his parents were advised to keep away from fish too, as Bobby reacted to the smell. Bobby is now twenty, and eats fish!

These days many children suffer from asthma. This is not only due to pollution and chemicals, but also due to all fast food, ice cream, soft drinks and other sweet goodies. Therefore, it is necessary to teach the child good and proper eating habits, with organic and fresh warm food. This will be valuable for a proper development of mind and body, and also valuable in preventing further recurrences of the illness.

Doctor Tenzin Choedrak treated a lady who had been suffering from chronic asthma for thirty years. About a year and a half after starting taking Tibetan medicines she was totally cured.

He also dealt with another lady who had breathing problems amounting to choking, for about twenty years. After one month on Tibetan medicines she had recovered markedly, and her blood pressure had come down.

Dr. Tamdin saw a patient who had suffered from sinusitis for 15-20 years. The patient had tried all sorts of allopathic medicines, but they gave no relief. After 45 days on Tibetan medicines, the patient was cured – his problems never returned.

Cancer

The solid foundation in Tibetan Buddhism, had contributed to a stableness of mind, which gave little room for cancer, in addition to an unpolluted environment and a healthy, unpolluted, traditional diet. So previously cancer scarcely existed in Tibet. But from ancient time, in the medical texts, it was described as one of the eighteen malignant illnesses that would appear in our time.

Now cancer is also a common disease in Tibet. Pollution due to the industrial activities, atomic waste and all that we know from our polluted Western world could be one of the reasons.

A more important reason is the constant psychic pressure under which the Tibetans are suffering. (See Appendix I)

According to Dr. Rapgay* who has psychological background, the classical doctor is engulfed in the cancerous growth, performs a biopsy, studies the material from the laboratory, takes X-rays, blood- and other analyses, and bases the treatment on what he finds – with the patient as a passive onlooker. The doctor is less concerned with the shock to the patient on learning he has cancer. The attitude of the doctor to the patient is essential for the patient to benefit from the treatment. He should change doctor if necessary, to one who can co-operate with the patient's diet, behaviour and thoughts, and show care for the whole being.

---

* For details see Appendix III

We have to deal with humans with thoughts, attitudes, feelings, food habits, living habits and biological functions, which are complex and difficult to sort out.

If we expect that cancer whose root cause lies in the mutual influence of these factors, can be separated from what this person is and does, and treat everyone in the same manner, we as therapists need to reconsider our approach.

Causes: The cancerous growth is the end product, a symptom. The real cause lies deeper. All healthy bodies carry organisms and bacteria that are harmful, even in a newborn, but the organisms live in peaceful coexistence with the body thanks to a good immune system. These organisms are very mobile and are found nearly everywhere in the body. Their activity is largely determined by many factors: genetic, diet, lifestyle, psychological, environmental and traumatic, but none of these factors can cause cancer on their own!

Thus the genetic cannot cause cancer in itself, but can make it more difficult to treat the disease.

A balanced diet is an essential factor, and is dependent on two items: what you eat, and the quality of the digestive system. In our time we are not conscious enough of what we eat. Fashion, taste and easiness determine the meals, and contain too much salt, meat, fat and sugar, in addition to substantial synthetic chemicals and additives.

More grains, fresh vegetables – especially green vegetables that contain more vitamins, minerals and proteins than other vegetables, fruit and fish, are essential.

Tobacco, alcohol and coffee should be completely avoided.

Exaggerated use of sugar and dairy products such as milk and ice cream can develop cancer in the upper region of the body, as their characteristics are parallel to the structures of the organs in the upper region.

Animal fat and strongly salted dairy products such as cheese, may affect the lower part of the body, while the combinations of both may affect the middle part of the body.

According to where the cancer is situated, the above-mentioned food items should be avoided. And in all cancer diseases, sugar, salt, fatty food, spicy and hot food should be reduced.

It is not enough just eating healthy and natural food. The digestive system must be fit to absorb the food and transport it in the right way to the blood cells and the tissue. The enzymes are responsible for breaking down the food, but it is just as important what condition the inner part of the digestive system is, whether it is inflamed or blocked. This is necessary for the absorbed food to pass satisfactorily through the system and be in a condition to supply nourishment to the cells. In addition it could also be that the body cells and the tissue themselves are not able to absorb the nourishment the blood brings them. Then the process stops, and residues build up in the cells and the tissue.

When we recommend a diet for the cancer patient, our main concern is the tumour – where is it located, what size it is, what are the secondary complications and how Wind, Bile and/or Phlegm are involved. Other factors are the age of the patient, the season and where he lives – in which part of the world, in which climate, the traditional diet of his culture. Naturally we also consider what the patient prefers within such a framework.

It has long been known that lasting stress usually weakens the immune system and makes it more vulnerable to viral and other infection. T-lymphocytes and certain blood cells are markedly reduced, and since it is their task to search out and destroy virus and bacteria, the lack of these increase the susceptibility to illnesses, such as cancer.

Genetic and traumatic sources: All the functions in the digestive system are closely related to the personality.

The inner part of the digestive system and the muscles in the organs are controlled by the autonomous nervous system, so that it produces digestive juices with ample acid, not only when a delicious meal is made, but also when one is angry or anxious.

When we are depressed, the inner part of the stomach becomes pale instead of red, less acid is produced, and we lose appetite. Anxiety, worry, disappointment, over work, or unintentional misuse (like the people who have a craving for spices, milk, tomatoes or whatever) can disturb the neatly balanced nerve mechanism that controls and synchronises the constant movement in the stomach and the intestines.

Regarding the complex relation between the hormone level, psychological stress and receptivity of cancer, E. Prederass, former president of the American Cancer Society, says: "Any one who has extensive experience with the treatment of cancer, is aware that there is a great difference among types of patients. I have personally observed cancer patients who have gone through a successful treatment and lived and been well for years. But then emotional stress such as loss of a son in war, infidelity of a daughter-in-law, or the burden of being out of work for a long period, reactivate the illness, with fatal results. There is solid evidence that the development of the illness itself is influenced by emotional sorrow".

Among the techniques to tackle the psychological factors are visualisation, meditation and certain types of Yoga or Qi Gong.

There is a lot in the environment we cannot avoid, such as global pollution. However, there are many things we can avoid. Such as food grown with artificial fertilisers, pesticides, artificial additives, gene manipulation, etc. This is a fast growing jungle in which one has to orientate oneself, not least through the sneaking gene manipulation.

We have two basic energy systems – one is related to metabolism and the endocrine system, which is characterised as Bile in Tibetan medicine, and the other is related to the nervous system and is responsible for the conscious and unconscious movements of the body.

When Pervasive Wind is out of balance, it can no longer prevent the organism being thrown out of control. The energies in the body are blocked, and the organisms take over the control of the cells and the reproductive activities of the body. Similarly, if Pervasive Wind is not disturbed, other factors cannot activate the process of illness.

As mentioned in the description of Wind, Pervasive Wind (See p. 10) assists all types of muscular movements and circulation. It has its seat in the heart, but goes to all parts of the body, the inner organs, the senses and distributes nourishment to the seven physical constituents.

Cancer is obviously a product of a complicated interaction between the neurological and the endocrine factors, and the emotions of the patient. How each organ in the body develops and functions is closely related to the nerve impulses and the nerve discharges. Messages, which pass via the nerves to each organ system, maintain an integrated activity in the organ.

When the messages become irregular, or the nerve pathways are broken, this can influence the organ if it is already under attack from illness promoting elements, and can induce a breakdown in the normal function.

If the pervasive energy cannot control further damage because it is influenced by illness, this can make it blind to what the mutant cells are doing, and permit them to multiply undisturbed or undiscovered. Since emotions are guided by Wind, it is so basically important to co-operate with the emotions of the patients, as in the case of Das.

Diagnosis: In Tibetan medicine we have a unique way of finding out the biological activities of the body in relation to the process of the illness, by studying the pulses and the urine.

> DAS, thirty years old, newly married, in a good job, is a good example. He had an advanced cancer of the gullet (oesophagus) and it was too late to operate. He got an appointment with Dr. Rapgay. Psychically he was completely shattered, physically he was emaciated and lost weight rapidly. He complained about pains in his chest, could not swallow, and regurgitated whatever he tried to eat. His pulse was weak, somewhat tense in the upper position, with a slight tremor.

> The heart pulse was irregular and disappeared on pressure – this is an important sign, as it ruled out any major cardiovascular disease. At the outset eight months ago, he had stomach problems and difficulties in swallowing food, and thus the doctor had only treated him for digestive problems.
>
> Das needed an assurance of what Tibetan medicine could do, and that it would only be effective if he changed his pessimistic attitude to the process of healing. When confidence and peace was established, we could sort out his diet, with his behaviour and with the psychological changes.
>
> Two weeks later Das came for a new appointment: No improvement. He had not been able to reconcile himself with his situation, and when he tried to start something, situations in the family prevented any development, and he was back to zero. Lost confidence in the medicines and no longer took them regularly.
>
> He was reassured and when he returned one month later, he was markedly better, and could also ingest some semi-liquid food. The most important thing that had happened, was that Das felt better as a person after he had started sharing responsibility to tackle the illness.

In Das' case, *the pulse beats* in the chest region were irregular, weak, somewhat tense, and clearly showed a state of inflammation. The liver and stomach pulses were weaker, and collapsed on pressure, and this gave two messages–

One, that the patient had a digestive problem, probably with disturbed emotional patterns. As this pulse was not as tense as the chest pulse, it told me that there was no greater organic disturbance in the liver or the stomach - it was therefore safe to believe that the liver and the stomach were secondary to the real problem.

Secondly, the immediate symptoms were strongly influenced by his emotions.

The examination of the urine disclosed a strong, foul smell, yellowish and somewhat murky. When it was stirred, it showed clear signs of inflammation with bubbles appearing irregularly in different sizes, which disappeared with a hissing sound. On closer examination some of the bubbles were very big and remained for a long time on the surface, clearly indicating an emotional condition.

Another variety of cancer indicating urine is a type of urine that shows a cold illness on one day and a warm illness on other days. One variety shows cracks in the oil-like surface of the urine. In other cases the urine is yellow and red and sticky.

According to Dr. Yeshi Donden*, the area of the tumour has a dirty colour.

In addition to these analyses, the mapping of the diet and lifestyle of the patient is a vital part of the diagnosis.

Treatment: There are a lot of herbs in Tibetan medicine that are specified for the different types of cancer, and the choice among them is decided by two factors:

First, which defects are involved – Wind, Bile and Phlegm and the combinations of them,

Secondly, where the illness is situated and which secondary complications are involved. This signifies, a patient with an active Wind – cancer in the abdomen will get quite a different medication to one with apparently the same illness, but where it is based on Bile and not on Wind.

The medicines are tailor-made for each patient. In the case of Das, the Wind symptoms were treated with individual diet and behaviour. The morning medicine was mild painkiller – the dose was increased later, when the Wind symptoms were under control. In addition he got a medicine against cancer that also eased the breathing function, and decreased inflammation and congestion in the throat and the upper digestive system.

Among these, many different minerals are especially effective to treat malignant tumours and other types of tumours. Most of the plant extracts are mainly used to complement the minerals and the animal extracts, and also

* For details see Appendix III

to neutralise any poisons or side effects of the medicines. In many cancer cases, we have seen that Tibetan medicines are effective, as well as where the patients have received chemotherapy and radiation.

Tibetan doctors have gained ever more attention for their ability to control and treat cancer, and have given many cancer patients relief the world over. Dr. Rapgay says: "I have personally observed patients of all age groups, who have improved markedly on Tibetan medicines. The cases of leukaemia have especially evoked interest. And independent of age group, patients with certain types of cancer have improved markedly after two to three months' treatment."

Another illustrating cancer case, was given by Dr. Yeshi Donden in an interview in the magazine *Mandala*:

> Some years ago, two brothers in India, the one in his twenties, the other in his forties, got cancer in the brain at the same time. The doctors recommended both of them to have an operation to remove the tumour. But their family could not afford two operations. The two brothers decided that the younger brother should take the operation, while the elder should try Tibetan medicine. For some time it looked like the younger brother managed well. So did the elder. But then a new tumour formed in the head of the younger, he needed another operation and died. The elder brother never took an operation, only Tibetan medicines and is now in his sixties.

Cancer is often a cold disease. For outer forms, such as skin cancer, breast cancer and nose cancer, a warm shower is actually recommended in Tibetan medicine.

For inner cancer it is important to drink a lot of boiled hot water.

The cancer patient should avoid stress, sleeping during the daytime, and too vigorous exercise.

> ROXANNE had breast cancer, was operated on, and re-operated on three years later, this time including chemotherapy and radiotherapy. However, a few years later the cancer had spread to the bones. She had to use morphine for the strong pain, got steadily worse and close to death.

As is often the case, many patients try other angles only when it is too late. Dr. Tsewang Tamdin was consulted, but only gave medicines for a few days, to see if anything could be done at that stage. Roxanne responded, and could slowly reduce the painkillers. The Tibetan treatment was followed up, and her health improved. five years later she could return to work.

A miraculous story? Perhaps. This is definitely not to say that Tibetan medicines can cure all cancers. The message it gives, is that it is always well worth a try.

Tibetan medicine differentiates among tumours on the inside, in the middle and on the outside of the body. However, a tumour on the outside does not only mean that it is on the surface of the skin, but also on the outside of the intestines, the liver, the pancreas, the stomach and the kidneys.

The middle tumours are found in the liver, the spleen, the kidneys and the urinary bladder.

The inner tumours are found on the inside of the stomach, the gall bladder, the large intestine and the lungs.

The outer tumours are the easiest to cure, then the middle, while the inner are more stubborn.

Multiple Sclerosis

This illness is related to the nervous system and the energy going through the meridians. There are thirteen meridians from the spine to the vital organs, and in Multiple Sclerosis (MS) these organs are influenced negatively due to blockages from the spine. It may have originated, e.g., from chronic fever, or after injuries and accidents. (We had a survey among our MS patients, asking them if they had experienced any neck or spinal injuries, or accidents in the past. The majority confirmed that they had, though for some it took some time to recall it, as the accident happened so many years ago.)

MS is connected to the body energy, often coupled to *the Wind type,* and is often of a cold nature.

But there can also be influences of *Bile*, as the liver and bile energies may have become too hot.

The *Phlegm* type may have problems in controlling urine, and problems of cold and digestion may be involved. They should avoid sour food, pickles, lactic acid food and drink, pure sweeteners, such as sugar. Also avoid cold, heavy food items, and food that induces Wind problems, such as coffee and tea, onions and garlic. Use salt sparingly.

Lamb and mutton, fish and grain foods, as well as boiled vegetables, are favourable. On the whole, cooked food, but not fried, smoked or salted, is recommended. Boiled, hot water is fine – especially after the meal for those who are thin. Keeping oneself warm is the key to all nervous disorders.

In Norway, MS has been given high priority in Tibetan medicine especially where the illness has not developed as far as the patient resorting to a wheel chair. Even though MS fluctuates in itself between good and bad periods, it looks like Tibetan medicines, and Tibetan acupuncture treatment, especially gold hammer (see p. 109) therapy, has a markedly good influence, and can delay the development of the illness. Some of the MS patients are actually symptom free, as long as they continue with the Tibetan medicines.

> KYLE had MS of a mild degree. As other MS patients he had increased liver functions, and some allopathic doctors thought that a high intake of herbal medicines might increase the liver functions even more. (This may be true if you use single herbs, but not with a balanced composition of herbs, as in Tibetan medicines). Kyle uses physiotherapy and osteopathy regularly, and this he says, eases the pain and the contractions in his chest. As a boy, he had two strong head injuries, and these old damages could definitely be part of the cause. After using Tibetan medicines for ten years, he tried to quit the medicines, only for a while. However, his condition was so good, that he did not need to return to the medicines.

MARTIN, 32 years old was very unsteady, with poor motor coordination, and severe problems of concentration. His MS was aggressive, and he soon ended up in a wheelchair. Forgot to take the medicines, and gave up. Tried again a couple of years later, with the same result.

ELLINOR, 21 years was unsteady, and had problems with concentration. After two years on Tibetan medicine, unsteadiness as well as concentration problems were reduced considerably, and now she is symptom free as long as she continues with the Tibetan medicines.

The Wind horse: Prayers are carried with the wind. Stands also for strength, speed, obedience and perseverance.

Headache

The causes for headaches are many and varied. This is the case according to Western, as well as to Tibetan methods of diagnosis. Among the various causes listed by Tibetan analyses are: fever, sinusitis, tension, lack of sleep, the predominance of bile, blood pressure alterations, low body resistance, intense menstruation, head injury and brain tumour.

The treatment of headaches with Tibetan medicine depends on the cause of the headache. Headaches will not be simply treated with painkillers. The Tibetan doctor identifies the cause through diagnostic tools such as urine and pulse analysis, and investigation into personal diet, behaviour and character.

Sinusitis: When a headache is due to sinusitis, the aim of the treatment is to clear the sinus cavities and reduce further build-up within the cavities.

Treatment consists of breathing exercises, diet regulation and a removal of the environmental irritant. Diet alteration involves reducing the intake of sweet food items, radishes, spinach, lentils, garlic, scallions and onions.

If the sinus irritant is tension or lack of sleep, these behavioural patterns should be altered, and less cold and raw foods eaten.

The sinuses may also be irritating because of allergy, pollution, dust and wind. In these cases the intake of coffee, tea, pork and carbohydrates should be reduced. The diet should be balanced and regular. And also one should be more aware of making an individual unsuitable diet restricted as long as possible.

Along with the sinus problems, bile imbalances may be encountered, producing indigestion and headaches. Occasionally these headaches are associated with vomiting.

Foods that should be avoided are rich and oily foods, nuts, milk products, and avocados, roasted and deep fried foods. These foods are difficult to digest if eaten in excess and late at night.

Blood Pressure: An increase in blood pressure may also lead to a throbbing headache. These headaches may be associated with an excessive accumulation of cholesterol or lipids in the blood.

In such cases, exposure to high temperatures or hot sun, spending time in a flexed position with the head down, depression and tension, may each lead to a headache.

To reduce the incidents of headache, it is necessary to reduce the intake of protein-rich foods, seafood and seafood products, salt, coffee, tea, alcohol and tobacco. It is also recommended to avoid excessive talking and thinking.

Low Body Resistance: A general reduction in body resistance may occur due to inadequate diet, heavy and prolonged menstruation or bleeding, high altitude and motion sickness. Poor digestion can lead to headaches and motion sickness can occur due to poor digestion. To reduce the occurrence of motion sickness, one ought to avoid foods that are too cold and avoid eating excessively. The abdomen should not be exposed, but fresh air will help to reduce the symptoms. Lack of oxygen at high altitudes may lead to altitude sickness and severe headaches. During menstruation, the reduction in blood within the body and to the brain may induce headaches.

Head Injury: Obviously, impact to the head may cause a headache due to the direct impact to the soft tissues of brain. However, sometimes headaches may occur many months after the date of impact due to brain contusion. Often it may not even be coupled to the injury by the patient. Tibetan medicine would be given to assist healing of the structures affected.

Brain Tumours: In the case of brain tumours, headaches are produced due to pressure on the brain, nerve and soft tissues in the surrounding area. Facial paralysis or numbness may occur. The headaches are frequent, often constant and severe, and are aggravated by physical and mental tension (Stress activates the brain). The headaches are often associated with vomiting, loss of vision and dizziness. In severe cases hemiplegia may occur (paralysis affecting one side of the face). Tibetan medicine, along with behavioural and dietary alterations, can be effective in reducing the size of the tumour. However the effectiveness of the treatment depends on the nature and size of the tumour, and on the individual's compliance.

Infection: Headaches may also be caused by infection, or by an increase in body temperature.

The treatment would again be to target the irritant causing the rise in body temperature, and to eliminate the infection.

Neck Pain: Arthritis in the neck, such as cervical spondylosis (stiffness and degenerative change in the neck bones) or osteoarthritis (mostly in middle-aged and elderly people, where the neck bones are stiff and inflamed), may lead to headaches as the circulation through the cervical spine to the brain may be reduced.

Muscular tension within the neck and shoulder region may also refer pain into the head that is perceived as headache. This may occur with cervical arthritis, tension or purely on account of poor posture.

It is also recommended to check eyesight.

One-sided Headache: The occurrence of one-sided headaches may be due to excessive toxins within the body, or to over-exposure to sun or heat. The headache is one-sided, the eyes water and an inability to tolerate bright light is apparent. It may also be associated with vomiting.

To summarise, the treatment of headaches by Tibetan medicine aims to identify and target the cause of the headache. By eliminating the cause of the headache through adjustment of diet, behaviour or environment (including climate in the office), and through taking Tibetan medication as required to alter the imbalance in personal humour or nature, the potential for headaches to re-occur is reduced.

Consists of a sceptre: Long life, power.
Uncoined silver: Wealth.
Writting pencil: Enlightement.

The Heart Problem

In Tibetan medical literature, the heart is considered to be the King of all the organs of our body system. And hence it is called *sNying* that is the essence of the whole body system.

Given the Tibetans' simple and contented life in addition to their practice of Buddhist philosophy of love and compassion, tolerance and forgiveness, major heart diseases were not common in Tibet prior to the Chinese occupation. However, after the Chinese occupation mental torture and trauma followed, and then several Tibetans in Tibet were found to be suffering from many heart ailments. Our former chief physician to His Holiness the Dalai Lama, late Dr. Tenzin Choedrak, never failed to mention the sudden prevalence of many cases of heart enlargement among the Tibetans in the Chinese concentration and torture camps, during his special teachings to our medical students and doctors.

Even in India, many of our Tibetan were also found to have many different ailments relating to their heart. They have been witnesses to the forceful and tragic occupation of Tibet, with killings, tortures, starvation, separation, escape, and the immediate hardships that they endured during their early days in exile.

In the modern world of today, particularly in the West, heart disease is widespread. This is due to stress and tension, fast and competing life styles that predominate in daily life, together with unwholesome diet, tobacco and pollution.

And this fast and competing culture of the West, together with rising stress and tension, exploitation and pollution has already started to take its toll in urban societies of India and other Eastern countries too, with a quantum leap in the cases of heart ailments. It is no wonder that heart disease has become a leading disease in our so-called modern society.

The heart is a repository of all positive and negative mental afflictions.

Among the positive mental factors are happiness, love, compassion. Among the negative mental factors are hatred, anger, anxiety, worry, depression and stress. They are all based and developed in the heart.

The nature and intricacies of heart and mind have intrigued our ancient spiritual masters and physicians for centuries. In fact, it can safely be said that the entire teachings of Tibetan Buddhist philosophy are centred on the study, analysis and development of heart and mind together. And no wonder. Heart plays a central role in the formation, development and existence of our human body and its health.

The all Pervasive Wind, one of the five subtypes of constitutional Wind, resides in the heart, circulates throughout our body and is responsible for many important physiological functions like movement, contractions, relaxation, and opening and closing of our sensory organs.

Tibetan medicine also believes that the essence of all our seven bodily constituents, namely essential food, blood, muscles, fats, bone, marrow and semen, called *Dhangs* (the radiance), pervades everywhere, though they reside in the heart. In these *Dhangs* lie the *prana* that is the life, aura and essence of health. Therefore, it is vital for Tibetan doctors to give attention to the heart and its normal functioning.

Causes: Anxiety, worry, mental disturbances, stress and tension, starvation, insomnia, strong hatred and anger are according to medical books the sources of immediate causes. They appear together with the original causes Wind, Bile and Phlegm with their afflictive emotions: desire, hatred and delusion.

Seven types of heart diseases:

1. *A type of depression,* with the following signs and symptoms:

Headache, forgetfulness, unnecessary disturbed feelings, thinking aloud, an attitude of withdrawal, intense fear on seeing unpleasant things, short breath, insomnia, a feeling of emptiness in the heart, pressure in the upper back, persistent pain and sensation at the mid-sternum point sixth and seventh vertebra.

At a later stage of the illness, patients will feel intense pain in the whole of the body, and some may even fall unconscious. If this type of illness is left untreated for a long time, it may result in insanity.

2. *Heart attack*:

2a: Giddiness, pain in the upper part of the back, gasping, dilation of blood vessels in the eyes, dryness and roughness in the mouth and on the tongue. The nature of the pulse is weak and empty.

2b. Dry, sharp pain like the stabbing of a dagger, bulging eyes, with rough panting and groans, palpitations, persisting pain in the front and the back of the left scapula, lingering pain in the left arm.

3. Fever in the heart:

3a: Hallucination, delirium, red eyes, pain in the upper back, a feeling of twisting in the heart, dry nostrils, heat (like burning fire) in the chest and the back. The pulse is rough and overflowing, the urine red-yellowish, and there is a black coating on the tongue.

3b: A burning sensation in the heart (like cutting into pieces), forgetfulness, confusion, dry and shortened tongue.

4. Fluid formation in the heart:

The patient is talkative, lacks sleep, feels fluttering in the heart, is yawning, and has mood swings.

5. Ischemic type of problem (not sufficient blood):

Forgetfulness, loss of appetite, heavy sleep and a sensation as though the heart is filled with stones.

6. Viral infection of the heart:

Clumsy, excretion of excess tears from the eyes, palpitation, delirium and a feeling of the heart being on a seesaw.

7. Schizophrenic type:

The pulse is empty; the patient has a fever, and is taciturn, or irritable, violent, with bulging eyes and suffers from headache.

Some of these are also subdivided further, in accordance with the upsetting of the three humoral energies of Wind, Bile and Phlegm. It is very difficult, though, to correlate each type of heart disease given above, with modern terminology.

In our clinical practice, we come across many major and common diseases of the heart, such as angina, ischemic heart disease, coronary arterial disease, arteriosclerosis, and also many congenital heart diseases.

Diagnosis: In Tibetan medicine it is very essential to identify properly the correct nature of the disease according to our classifications, before giving the required medicines. In our medical text it is mentioned, that by mistaking smoke for vapour, and snake for a rope, we can make mistakes in diagnosing diseases that have similar physical signs and symptoms, thereby giving wrong medications leading to fatal consequences. Tibetan doctors have to enquire about the case history of the patient, examine his eyes, tongue, urine and pulse.

Eyes may be reddish when there is a strong heart disease of Bile nature, Pale and watery when Phlegm is involved, Dry and rough in the case of Wind. Also, a stiff look and fearful eyes may suggest some deep emotional disturbances or schizophrenic type of heart problems.

Similarly, a reddish *tongue* signifies a Bile association with the heart illness, a pale and a moist tongue if Phlegm is involved, And bluish, with cuts and cracks in the tongue in the case of Wind.

Careful examination of *the pulses* is the secret to a perfect understanding of the nature of the disease. The pulse can be very weak and sinking in the case of ischemic heart disease, very strong and overflowing in the case of an enlarged heart, and some serious heart problems needing immediate care. Absence of pulse beat in the right or left hand, in the index, middle or ring finger, may indicate some severe blockage in the arteries and veins in a particular organ or location.

Tibetan doctors are taught to pick up the right signals from the different characteristics of the pulse, to identify their pathological nature, the severity and the prognosis. No wonder that it needs great experience and sharp mental expertise to come to the right diagnosis. Similarly, *urine analysis* too gives a great deal of information as to the hot and cold nature of the heart problem.

Yellowish and reddish urine indicate some heart problems with Bile association, Whitish urine indicates Phlegm, and watery and bluish urine signifies Wind.

In addition to the different colours of the urine, one has to look for the size of the bubbles, how they appear and disappear, the smell of the urine; its transparency (clouds) and the sediments, to further ascertain the various complications and prognosis of the disease.

Treatment: In the treatment of heart diseases, we have found that the Tibetan herbal pills are particularly effective in controlling angina and ischemic heart problems, without any unwelcome side effects.

But cases like coronary arterial disease and arteriosclerosis need more time and careful observations. We find that the response of some patients from this disease category is very encouraging, but we still do not know how far the medicines are effective in dissolving the fatty deposits.

There are sizeable numbers of our Indian patients who depend mainly on Tibetan medicines' care and management after their major heart surgeries.

Furthermore, we have numerous clinical records to prove that the Tibetan medicines have helped greatly in many chronic cases of heart ailments, where patients did not find any desired relief from modern conventional medicines.

However, this is not to say that Tibetan medicines have sure remedies for every kind of heart disease. Particularly when it comes to some congenital heart diseases like valve defects and holes in the heart, it has no reliable medicines to give.

On the other hand, for cases like severe mental depression, emotional disturbances, and schizophrenic type problems, moxabustion at specific meridians of the heart gives great relief. In some severe cases of angina pain, even cupping with bronze cups gives immediate relief from the pain.

Venesection or blood letting, though not often practised in India, can be lifesaving and has been reported to give a quick and desirable relief from some form of inflammations of the heart with high fever, and also against severe pain resulting from blockages in the heart, etc.

Also hot fomentation and some form of warm massage at the specific meridians of the heart, are found to be extremely helpful in terms of giving temporary relief, and also as a preventive measure.

Diet and life style always plays a vital role in the treatment and management of heart problems. Excess intake of sweet or sour foods, fatty or deep fried foods should be avoided. Also, heavy alcoholic drinks and strong black tea and coffee should be discouraged.

Regularised exercises, deep breathing exercises, relaxation therapies and some simple meditation with chanting or prayers are also reported to be of great help.

Shaping one's mind with the positive attitude, spiritual belief and meditation, compassion, forgiveness and tolerance are also keys to the care and maintenance of one's most precious organ called heart. And this is how our former Chief physician to His Holiness the Dalai Lama, the late Dr. Tenzin Choedrak had demonstrated perfectly how to keep his heart and mind in balance to overcome nearly seventeen years of total imprisonment with untold physical sufferings and mental agonies.

In any kind of disease, and particularly in the case of heart disease, the approach of treatment is more important than administrating the medicines themselves, and given the right type of medicines, it is essentially more vital than giving any strong suppressive drugs. And certainly, it is more rewarding and body friendly.

Skin Disease

The skin is the largest organ of the body, with millions of pores that help to regulate the body's temperature. The skin protects the body from being invaded by bacteria, and is the most sensitive organ for outer stimuli. We change skin tissue all the time, while the skin cells get their nourishment from the inner cell metabolism.

As the skin is our main secretion organ and our most sensitive organ, it tells us about the condition of our health and is important for diagnosis. For example, with chronic tiredness the skin of the face becomes dry, pale and without clarity. Such a sign indicates a Wind imbalance, which influences the psychological as well as the physiological condition.

If Wind imbalance is the cause, the affected skin is rough and dark brown. If Bile imbalance is the cause, the patient loses his body hair and the affected area of the skin becomes red and gives a burning sensation. If Phlegm imbalance is the cause, this gives irritation in the skin, and the affected area is pale and thick. The Tibetan name of a Bile skin disease stems from the symptoms that appear. The skin reminds one of the neck of a pulling ox, with hard and thick skin with pimples. Clinically the skin is red and thickened, or with dark pimples with a scaly surface, often identified as psoriasis. It is often caused by alcohol, sour or pungent food taken in extreme, and can also be due to strenuous work in strong heat. This illness tends to appear in the neck or the back of the head. In its first stage the skin is irritated, with eruptions of small pimples, which by and by develops into flat pimples of varying size. The dead skin cells fall off when one scratches the area, and the skin beneath becomes dark red, with blood oozing out.

Tibetan doctors say that our mental condition and the healthy condition of the skin are closely related. According to Tibetan medicine, Wind is the medium that combines body and mind. They say that the formation of skin, nerves and brain from the ectoderm cells support this concept.

The low excretion of the oily substance *sebum*, gives a dry skin surface. This waste of fat cells can also be explained with an imbalance in Wind. There is also a direct connection between ageing and worsening of Wind, due to loss of fat cells, as one grows older.

A parallel to the aspect of the skin is the tongue, which is important in Tibetan and Chinese diagnosis. A healthy person has a red, soft, wet and flexible tongue. Healthy skin is also soft, wet and elastic.

In Tibetan medicine the skin is also regarded as the gate to acute illnesses at their outset, and as the gate to chronic illnesses in their final stage. Symptoms such as chills, extreme sweat, skin that is too oily, eruptions, etc., is a warning, so that one can avoid getting worse. Dark rings under the eyes, facial wrinkles too early on, itching skin, irritation anywhere on the body, and dry surface skin indicate a chronic illness or poisoning in the blood system, which has been stored in the body for years, until it feels forced to erupt. Psoriasis is a typical example.

The skin tells you whether you are in physical and psychical balance, but many overlook the skin's signals, when it is telling you that there is an imbalance in the physical interior and the psychological condition. In Tibetan medicine all negative emotions such as sorrow, fear, anxiety, depression and aggression are basic causes that will reduce our physical radiation, via the skin.

Thus it is not sufficient to treat the skin with ointments and oils, but with the right diet, lifestyle and environment. In order to have healthy skin it is vital we eat healthy food, get enough rest and relaxation, and have a positive mind. The psychological part is as important as the physical – the brain and the mind also need rest. A good philosophy of life is an essential factor for a cure.

When Wind is mainly responsible for skin problems, massage with, for example, sesame oil is recommended. After the massage with oil, the skin should be rubbed with barley flour to counteract Wind, to get a clear skin, and it also helps to break up fatty tissue.

When Phlegm is mainly responsible for skin problems, sun bathing is recommended, followed by a strong massage.

When the cause is a complication .because of chronic illnesses, medicines are needed, in addition to medicinal baths.

Some of the medical plants used for skin treatment, are sandalwood, saffron, hibiscus, abelmoschus moschustus, bitter long pepper, black pepper, ginger, calmus root (acorus calamus), rubia cordifolia, clove (syzigum aromaticum), azadirachta indica, asparagus, raphanus sativus, Indian sesame, turmeric (gurkuma longa), berberis aristata, mountain thistle (saussarea lappa) and Tibetan hippopha

Types: Skin problems are due to either too strong growth of micro organisms, too much body fluid, mental disturbances, imbalances in the three principles Wind, Phlegm and Bile.

Formation of skin spots without pigment that can resemble *vitiligo* (leucoderma). This is considered a very infectious illness, mostly due to spreading of serous fluid in the sub skin. Microorganisms may also be the cause. The most serious of this type of skin disease can lead to malign diseases in the skeleton, or to leprosy that only affects the skin. Vitiligo is a skin disease that develops into white spots on the skin. They occur mostly on the forehead, around the eyes and on the lips, but can appear anywhere on the body. In Tibetan medicine this illness has been known and treated for 2500 years.

The illness arises because there is an imbalance between the body fluids and bacteria, in relation to the three energies Wind, Bile and Phlegm.

The main mechanism of the blood serum is to transport the essential nutrition after the three stages of digestion: Breaking down of the food particles, digestion and cleansing, to the liver, and through the nine channels to all parts of the body. In the liver the colour forming Bile is made, but when complications arise in this forming, Vitiligo will develop in the serum.

Serum: Serous fluid exists everywhere in the body, but of concern is that found especially in skin pigmentation and in the joints. In the gall bladder an imbalance of serous fluid formed from the bile and blood that is still impure after cleansing, together with the imbalance in colour regulating Bile and skin cleansing Bile leads to vitiligo.

According to which of the three energies Wind, Bile and Phlegm that is most prominent, the illness can be divided into several groups:

Vitiligo due to Wind imbalance feels rough and is purple or dark coloured.

Vitiligo due to Bile imbalance has a reddish colour with localised white spots or loss of body hair, accompanied by a burning sensation. The white spots spread quickly.

Vitiligo due to Phlegm imbalance gives itching, and white spots that spread slowly.

White spots can also be due to scalded skin or wounds from old burns, be side effects after strong medication with antibiotics, or through strongly infested blisters.

In children the white spots can arise due to wrong diet or care, or because of strong medication during the mother's pregnancy.

Treatment: The medicines are given according to the patient's character, and for subduing inflammations of Bile and blood serum. According to Dr. Tamdin's experience the treatment gives results in 60% of the cases, apart from where the white spots are due to burns or scalds.

The patient should avoid sour food, vinegar, soy sauce, cold milk, unripe fruit, sweets, unripe yoghurt, food with a very hot potency – especially spices, strong tea, oily and fatty food and too much salt. He should eat balanced and regular meals. The patient should avoid clothes with synthetic fibres.

Warts: They are usually white, but under the soles of the feet they are described as black. The wart can be burnt directly with the glow of the tip of *Rubia Cordifolia*.

In its first stage the skin is white and scaly, it itches, and when the patient scratches, blood and a clear white fluid oozes out. In an early stage blisters appear on the head, near the nostrils, around the mouth and on arms and legs, which develop into a yellowish outer skin that itches and oozes fluid, with pus. At the next stage, there is loss of hair, and the skin cracks, often with boils. This illness appears most often in the summer and the autumn.

Most often due to wrong dietary habits, increased body weight or specific infections boils discharge pus and fluid. In the first stage small boils appear on the head, arms and legs or around the nostrils and the mouth. The boils become infected and develop into sores, while the skin becomes coarse and cracked. It is accompanied by a warm or cold sensation with itching.

> Steven, four years had atopic eczema. Little Steven suffered badly, the parents lost sleep as he was crying and scratching all night, and the hospital had no more to offer. With Tibetan medicines he got rid of the itching and the eruptions, but as soon as he stopped the medicines, the eczema returned. Combined with some lymph drainage, the eczema disappeared after two years, and his asthma also improved.

> Eva, 42 years suffered from atopic eczema: The face was completely covered with eczema. She felt it was really unsavoury to look at. After two years on Tibetan medicines the skin was smooth and flawless, and she sent portraits to show "before" and "after", which was forwarded to Dr. Wangyal as referred to earlier.

> Peter, seven years, had eczema. His body was covered in eczema. Two years later the skin was smooth and spotless, but he had to continue with one of the medicines.

Diabetes

In Tibet, diabetes is little known, but is widely spread in India. This is due to the Indian diet consisting of a lot of sweet ingredients. Diabetes is usually connected to too much salt, sweet, cool and heavy food, and a prolonged stay in wet and humid places. This increases Phlegm and fat in the body, which slowly joins the urine, which is gathered in the urinary bladder. Here it is excreted, with several characteristics in the urine – urine types.

Types of diabetes: Tibetan medicine classifies three types of diabetes, where Wind (that controls movement) is prominent, where Bile (that controls heat) is prominent, and where Phlegm (that controls the body fluids) is prominent.

These types are further divided into twenty subtypes, which are determined according to colour and matter in the urine. For your curiosity, below is the information on how the Tibetan doctors can diagnose diabetes through the analysis of the urine:

The ten Phlegm subtypes:

(i) As water (the urine is clear, without colour and resembles water)
(ii) As wine (the surface is clear, but with thick sediment)
(iii) As sugar cane juice (the urine is sticky, brown and very sweet)
(iv) Thick (the urine is thick and white with a little "hair" overnight)
(v) As rice flour (the urine is white like rice flour)
(vi) As semen (the urine looks like that, or as if it is mixed with semen)
(vii) Like sand (the urine sample has a strong smell and contains sand-like particles.)
(viii) Cool (the urine is plentiful, sweet and cold)
(ix) Slow (a little sample of urine at a time, and very slow urination)
(x) As saliva.

The six Bile subtypes:

(i) Like toasted barley (as a solution of toasted barley)
(ii) Ink (black)
(iii) Blue (clear blue)
(iv) As extract of Rubia cordifolia (the urine smells foul and is vaguely red)
(v) Like Berberis aristata (the urine is yellow, bitter

or pungent)

(vi) Like blood (the urine is red as blood, with a strong smell and salty taste)

The four Wind subtypes in the urine:

(i) Marrow (the urine is mixed with marrow)

(ii) Fat (the urine is mixed with fat)

(iii) Elephant urine (the urine is thick, yellow and flows continuously without pressure)

(iv) Honey (the urine is sweet, dark yellow and resembles honey)

Symptoms are insomnia, profuse sweat, bad body smell, quick growth of hair and nails, sweet taste in the mouth, dry palate and throat. The patient prefers a cool environment and is craving for cool food. He has a burning sensation in the palms of the hands and feet, and dark urine, which attracts flies.

These symptoms confirm that the patient has got diabetes. Different colours in urine can also indicate other illnesses. Other symptoms are:

Phlegm symptoms: Digestive problems, anorexia, extreme sleepiness, profuse production of sputum, vomiting.

Bile symptoms: Pain in the genital organs and the urinary bladder, dry mouth, superficial fever, diarrhoea, the patient can develop a tendency to epidemic fever.

Wind symptoms: Heart palpitation, insomnia, difficulty in breathing, tremors, shooting pains, exaggerated feeling of hunger and exaggerated production of sputum.

All the twenty types of diabetes should be treated in their initial stages, if not, there will be complications with ten types of skin eruptions.

These ten eruptions mostly appear on the joints, vital points and in muscular tissue, in the case of diabetes:

1. Like an earthen bowl (protruded edges and flat in the middle)

2. Like a tortoise (there is strong pain inside the eruption, and it is spread over a large area. It is smooth and resembles a tortoise shell)

3. Bent (big eruption with serious infections and pain, appears mostly on the back and the stomach.)

4. Like a web (hard and covered like a web of veins)

5. Like ringworm (insufferable pain, with breakage and red spots)

6. Like lentils (the eruption is hard, ripens with difficulty, and resembles the shape and size of lentils.)

7. Like mustard (quickly ulcerates, with strong pain and inflammations, surrounded by an eruption resembling mustard seeds.)

8. Like vidor (belonging to the juniper family) (is very hard and spherical in shape)

9. Like a bubble (a big eruption surrounded by many small, which resemble bubbles)

10. Like inner malign tumours (swelling and inflammation as in malign tumours)

Treatment: In the initial stage it is important to treat Phlegm and fat accumulation to remove the urine type symptoms. Food and drink should have a light and coarse quality, stored grain, meat of dry land animals, light exercise and a light fasting is recommended. Milk products and bread with barley flour is also favourable. So is good exercise, and avoid sleeping during the daytime. Rubbing and massage with, for example, lentil powder, is very good.

Initially a general Tibetan medicine is used. Then specific medicines as to which defects are involved:

For the Phlegm type: The treatment starts by cleansing with emetics, to be followed up by other medicines for Phlegm.

For the Bile type: The treatment starts by cleansing with purgatives, followed by meat soup from game. Then medicines for Bile are added.

For the Wind type: The treatment starts with a mixture of medicinal herbs and butter.

For Phlegm and Bile the medicines are taken together with honey. Honey is favourable. Even though it is sweet, it changes its character during the digestive process, where the taste becomes bitter and astringent. The honey must be produced without feeding the bees with sugar.

Skin eruptions due to complications are treated by drinking goat's urine and further treated as sores.

The increase of Phlegm and fat in the body means that there is too much, or an accumulation of unused glucose. Phlegm is a body principle that is dominated by the Earth and Water elements, and these two together produce Sweet taste.

Sweet taste is what you find in all grains, in meat – specially pork, in sweet fruits, potatoes, carrots, cold milk, and sweet and sour fruit juices. It is therefore easy to conclude that too much sweet creates imbalance. Which further leads to poor digestive heat. If this condition is allowed to continue, the consequence will be disturbances in the kidneys and then the urinary bladder, it will give pain in the hips and waist area, and cold feet. The kidneys are the main seat for the Phlegm principle, and therefore especially at risk by Phlegm imbalance.

Pure honey is the exception, because, as mentioned above, though it is sweet in taste, it changes taste to bitter and astringent during the digestive process. Thus honey reduces Phlegm and is recommended both in the diet and as a transport together with the herbal medicines.

Tibetan medicine also considers honey favourable for reducing obesity (where Phlegm-fluid is part of the syndrome.) Barley and meat from animals living in dry areas are also beneficial.

Loss of insulin production in the pancreas, which helps the body cells to absorb blood sugar and gives energy to the body, can be compared to loss of digestive heat destroying the regulation of sweet taste in the digestive system and in the blood, in the Tibetan theory.

The *Wind* type should follow the following diet and behaviour: Avoid too much goat's meat and products, pork, coffee, strong tea, avoid excessive fasting, avoid stress and strain due to deep sorrow or to strong mental activity, loss of weight, excessive sunbathing, cold chills, laziness, resist too much wind in the intestines, seek light elements in life to avoid depression, seek warmer areas.

It is beneficial to use cardamom, for instance as tea in the morning or the evening, and turmeric in the afternoon.

The *Bile* type should avoid too much meat, butter, molasses, alcohol and beer. They have problem with yellow skin, faeces and urine, and of insomnia, headache, diarrhoea, poor appetite.

It may be beneficial to take Terminalia chebula (an Asiatic stone-fruit) in the morning or at midday, and Emblica officinalis (resembles gooseberries) in the evening, if the symptoms as mentioned earlier prevail.

The *Phlegm* type should avoid too much fat and raw food, get enough exercise. The patient suffers easily from cold, has too weak digestive heat, suffers from wind in the intestines, has a pale skin, limbs and joints feel unstable, is drowsy, sleeps too much, has breathing difficulties, has too much discharge from the nose, has difficulties in stretching the limbs, puts on weight easily. The body heat is generally too weak. Then the body does not manage to absorb the essential nourishment from food, or discharge the residues at the right time.

With Phlegm, cardamom is also beneficial morning and evening, and Emblica officinalis in the afternoon.

In chronic cases there can be sores on the reproductive organs. Other problems are a weak sensation in the limbs, extreme thirst and loss of sight.

For the diabetes patients who also have heart and blood vessel problems, or have problems with alcohol, it is also necessary to treat the impure blood. One who drinks too much alcohol can damage the liver, which loses its ability to store enough nourishment, as sugar, for further use. This may end with death. The patient may in addition be extremely sleepy. There are many possibilities within Tibetan medicine for purifying the blood, or help the liver function before the onset of diabetes.

MRS. SHAW, who had diabets for more than twenty years, got a large swollen sore on her back, oozing matter. This type of sore is normally difficult to cure. But with Tibetan medicines not only did her sore heal, but also did several other black spots. And her diabetes became normal.

MRS. PALMER, sixty years, had high blood pressure, blood sugar and gout. She started with Tibetan medicines after a long period with allopathic and homeopathic medicine. To start with her gout felt worse, before it eased. The blood pressure and the blood sugar became stable, and she felt fitter.

MRS. RICHARDS had diabetes for two years when she started with Tibetan medicines. She was completely cured and there are now no traces of the diabetes.

MRS. HOLLAND had diabetes for nearly last twenty years. She used allopathic medicine, and needed two insulin injections daily. Immediately after she started taking Tibetan medicines, she could drop the insulin injection. The level of blood sugar was normalised.

Miracles can obviously also happen with "old" diabetes! It is very beneficial to start the treatment with Tibetan medicines as early as possible. Dr. Choedrak and other Tibetan doctors stress that diabetes is difficult to cure, but Tibetan medicine can at any rate improve the condition.

A symbol of "freedom from restraint"

AIDS

As early as in eighth century, in the Tibetan book on medicine it was predicted that in the time of Kali-Yuga – the time we live in now – there will be a period of degeneration. Man will indulge in many kinds of vices, in thought, in words and in deeds.

Well, man has always done, more or less. But today war and violence is worldwide. Pollution from industry and agriculture, atomic explosions and accidents, deforestation and spreading deserts disrupt the balance globally and locally. According to the Tibetan book on medicine, *Guyshi,* this is the cause of the illnesses of our time.

After the Chinese occupied Tibet, they established their industry, their atomic plants, their depot of atomic residue, and started heavy deforestation. Their regime has up to this day resulted in a loss of 1.2 million Tibetans, where at least every tenth Tibetan has been in prison with torture and political brainwashing. There is a suppression of religion and culture to a degree we cannot fathom.

With physical pollution and psychic stress as new factors, cancer and other "civilised" illnesses have appeared, and spread. Before 1951 cancer did not exist in Tibet. AIDS had by 2002 not yet reached Tibet, this is still a young scourge in this part of the world. Tibetan medicine sees AIDS too as a result of the time we are living in, with imbalance on many levels.

Tibetan doctors consider that a virus causes AIDS and this virus is a result of chemical pollution and environmental imbalance.

Sinbhu: According to Tibetan medicine the body has 84,000 *Sinbhu* – nucleus cells – that fight illness and maintain good health. The AIDS virus settles in these cells, where they stay dormant.

When the body is exposed to wrong diet, blood loss, excessive sex with vigorous emptying of semen, of great stress or displeasure with life, the vital energy becomes too low, and the AIDS virus becomes active. The 84,000 cells that normally fight illness turn against the body and attack.

Dhang: When the temperaments Wind, Bile and Phlegm are in balance, they strengthen the vital essence, *Dhang,* through the digestive system. The vital essence is the subtle, clear and luminous fluid in the central channel in the heart.

This central channel, which is luminous, is the main seat for the subtle energy system that is the base of the coarse anatomy of the body. Through the main canal and the side canals that flow from it like the veins in a leaf, the vital essence flows together with the Wind energy and the conscience. The Wind energy and conscience follow *Dhang* through the subtle drainage system of the body as a clear liquid.

Dhang is far more important than consciousness, the Wind energy or channels. It is the end product of the regenerative liquid, which is responsible for the continuation of life and for the healthy condition, healthy look and vitality. It is the end product of the systematic digestive cycle – from intake till excretion, the taking up of nutrients in the liver, its transformation into blood, which is transformed into fat, bone, marrow, renewed fluid – in the end *Dhang*.

The elements: The vital essence goes through a change, when attacked by the AIDS virus in the 84,000 cells, depending on the basic nature of the cells. That is to say, according to the temperament they belong to Wind, Bile or Phlegm, plus blood, which direct the metabolism. Matter is by its nature formed by the five elements – Earth, Water, Fire, Wind and Space.

Muscles and bones consist mainly of the element Earth, the body liquids of the element Water, the body heat of the element Fire, the air in the body (what moves) like sensual breath to the many subtle currents of energy, of the element Wind, and the cavities of the body of the element Space.

Temperaments: Even though this is a repetition of what has been written earlier in this book, each doctor has his way of expressing it, which broadens our understanding:

Wind is a subtle energy that directs the movements in the body – as breath, movement in the muscles and tissue. It expels mucus, saliva, sweat, urine, and faeces, causes circulation in the heart and in the blood vessels, deals with all expansions and contractions. This is formed by the Wind element.

The *Bile* energy is the heat energy. It directs digestion, absorption, metabolism, body temperature, skin colour, intelligence and understanding. This is formed by the Fire element.

The *Phlegm* energy is a fluid formed by the Earth and Water elements. This energy supplies the material for the physical structure and is responsible for the firmness of the body. It lubricates the joints, gives a stable mind, gives skin its humidity and makes it soft and shining.

These three temperaments are mutually dependent. When they are out of balance, one of them can dominate a given cell among the 84,000 *Sinbhu*.

Which energy is thrown out of balance, is dependent on the person's individual physiology, diet and behaviour. As the cells' Wind, Bile and Phlegm energies get into an increasingly stronger imbalance the AIDS virus starts to attack the main tissues of the body, slowly and progressively.

The *Wind* dominated cells strike the joints, skin, intestines and hips.

The *Bile* cells in imbalance strike the stomach, head and skin.

The *Phlegm* cells in imbalance first strike the chest, then the lungs, large intestine and brain.

AIDS symptoms which are based on *Wind*, is headache in one half of the head, debility, emaciation, weakened nerves, loss of weight, and sometimes incoherent speech and thought, or loss of both. In addition the two other energies will also come into imbalance, as well as the blood. This will cause many secondary infections, which may resemble symptoms of cancer, stroke, leprosy and brain disturbances.

AIDS symptoms that are based on *Bile*, are nausea, headache, confusion, heaviness in body and mind, diarrhoea, stomach problems, fever and a yellowish complexion.

AIDS symptoms that are based on *Phlegm*, Anorexia, digestive trouble, loss of taste, loss of body heat, exaggerated sputum, swollen eyes and a greyish complexion.

Treatment: Depending on which temperaments are involved, different medicines will be advised to restore balance, strengthen the immune system and the metabolism.

In the diet the following must be reduced drastically: Salt, sweet and sour, yeast, pork, coffee, strong tea, and alcohol.

Concerning lifestyle, stress must be avoided, and sex life modified. Positive thoughts, meditation, and exercise in fresh air are important factors.

The peony: The flower of spring

APPENDICES

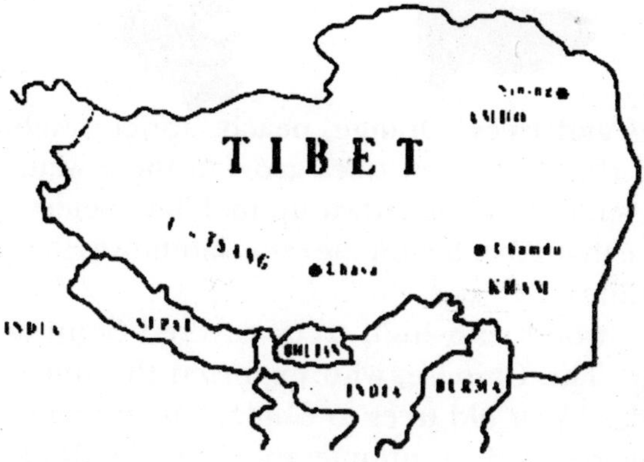

Appendix I

TIBET: CULTURE AND FATE

For many people Tibet is a fairyland – a Shangri-la. Many know that H.H. the Dalai Lama had to flee Tibet, and that China controls the country. Many know that the Dalai Lama received the Nobel Peace Prize in 1989. A few know a little more, but for most a great deal is unclear. It may therefore be of value to tell you a little about Tibet – that too gives perspective to the Tibetan medical culture.

Tibet is a majestic country in the heart of Asia. It is one of the most important countries in the world ecologically and climate-wise. The Tibetans call their country the third pole, after the North and the South Pole. It covers 2.5 million square meters that is equivalent to 2/3 of India, or most of Europe. Average height above the sea is 3,650 meters. Several of its mountains in the Himalayas rise more than 8,000 meters. The Tibetan plateau is the highest in the world. Tibet is wild and barren as well as fertile. Dry in the West, humid in the East, and fertile in the valleys in between, along the rivers.

Plants and trees: Orange, peach, apricot, walnut trees and high rhododendron trees grow in the lowland (about 3,500 meters). Barley is grown up to 4,500 meters. – We do not realise that Tibet lies on the same latitude as the southern Mediterranean.

Dense wood with high trees covered Southern Tibet especially. The Chinese, who exported the timber of the two hundred year old trees to China, has laid most of these bare. This resulted in innumerable large landslides of soil during the monsoon, and is one of the main causes of the recurrent floods in China, Bangladesh, Laos, and Vietnam.

The woods of Tibet cover more than 25 million hectares. Most of the trees grow on steep hills, with more than 35° slopes in the river valleys of the Southeast. The most common types are tropical and subtropical conifers: Pine, fir, Mediterranean pine, larch and cypress. The most common deciduous trees are oak and birch. The woods are old, with trees over 200 years old. On an average, the thickness of the forests was in total 273 m3 per hectare, while the U-Tang area in Central Tibet, up to 2,300 m3. This is the thickest pine tree growth in the world.

As part of the "development" more than 70,000 Chinese workers, in the Southeast alone, hewed large woods. In some areas more than 80% of the woods were cut down (1999). In 25 years timber worth more than 54 billion dollars has been felled and exported.

Understanding this, the Chinese authorities have started reforestation.

Only when the last tree is hewn,
Only when the last river has been poisoned,
Only when the last fish has been caught,
Only then will we discover that we cannot eat money.

Cree Indian forecast.

More than 100,000 species of plants and trees grow in Tibet, many among them endemic and rare. Rhododendrons alone consist of 400 species, about half of all rhododendron in the world.

Among these plants are about 2,000 different medicinal plants, which are used in Tibetan as well as Chinese and Indian medicine. We are mostly focused on the rain forests of the world, but the flora and fauna of Tibet are just as important to us!

Birds: In Tibet there are 532 differentiated species of birds, divided into 57 groups, which is more than 70% of the total for China. Among them storks, wild swans, Blyth's kingfishers, geese, ducks, beach birds, brown breasted jungle flycatcher, finches, large beaked bush warblers, wagtails, grey sided thrush, bearded vulture, woodpeckers, jays, eagles, falcons, and the most famous of them all – the rare black neck crane.

Wild animals: The mountains and woods of Tibet have been the home for many rare and threatened wild animals. Some are extinct, and some have only a few representatives left, such as the snow leopard, the giant panda and the red panda. Still left are lynx, sky leopard, black bear, brown bear, wild yak, blue sheep, musk ox, golden ape, wild ass, Tibetan gazelle and antelope, Himalayan mouse hare and others.

Before the Chinese invasion, hunting wild animals was strictly forbidden. The Chinese on the other hand, actively encouraged trophy hunts of threatened species. Rare Tibetan animals such as the snow leopard were hunted for the value of its skin and sold for large sums on the international market. Hunting license for the rare Tibet antelope was USD 35,000 and for the argali sheep USD 23,000 (1999). Hunters killed herds of antelope, gazelle, blue sheep and wild yak. The meat was sold to China, Hong Kong and Europe. According to a Chinese researcher (1995), 81 species are threatened in Tibet, among them 39 mammals, 37 bird species, four amphibians and one snake.

In 1998 there were only 1,000 wild pandas left. China has monopolised the giant panda, and shows them off to other countries as a political gesture.

What about the Yeti – the abominable snowman – does it exist? The researchers have been searching for it, and the Tibetans allege that it does exist, but it knows how to hide.

Minerals: Security is very low. Many workers are killed, or get great health problems. Tibet has large deposits of 126 different minerals, which include a substantial part of the world's reserves of gold, lithium, uranium, chrome, copper, borax and iron. The Chinese run the mines intensively, which increases the danger of landslides of earth and stones, a massive erosion of soil, loss of habitat for wild animals and birds, and pollution of streams and rivers.

It is expected that seven "key" minerals will be totally exploited within a few years. Tibet has the world's largest reserve of high graded uranium. The oil fields of Amdo (North Tibet) produce more than one million crude oil per year — these are many titbits for China!

Rivers: Tibet is the source of many of the biggest rivers in Asia, such as the Indus, Brahmaputra, Sutlej, Karnali, Salween, Mekong, Yangtse and Huang. They end up in China, India, Pakistan, Nepal, Bhutan, Burma, Bangladesh, Thailand, Vietnam, Laos and Cambodia. These rivers and their branches are the nerve centres for millions in Asia and they sustain 47% of the world population. Thus it is vital for the entire world that this system is preserved.

The massive deforestation, mining, and intensive agriculture cause strong erosion of the soil. The devastating floods that result destroy the possibility of sustenance for the farmers in the countries the rivers run through, in addition to washing away people and villages. The rains, due to the destabilised climate, enlarge the floods. China's own estimates show that 120,000 m2 in China and Tibet alone have turned into deserts due to human activity, by 1999.

The help given to Tibet by the industrial world is totally misunderstood. Support from the World Bank for large industrial projects is like honey to the Chinese, tens of millions of dollars per year. One project in 1999, supported by the World Bank, was for immigration of nearly 70,000 Chinese!

One of the biggest attacks on nature in Tibet was the building of an electricity plant at Yamdro Tso, a vast lake that is a very holy site for the Tibetans. The entire lake will dry up, as will the much needed water sources. 16% of the agricultural land in the area is swallowed up by the project. What drinking water is available, results in diarrhoea, loss of hair and skin problems.

The monsoon rain is as important to Asia as it is to Africa. The Chinese activities on the Tibetan plateau have influenced the jet streams that blow across it. This is thought to be a source of the typhoons in the Pacific and to El Niño and La Niña.

So the world as a whole is influenced by what happens on the Tibetan high plateau.

The nomads: The barren highlands are where the nomads live, with their yak and sheep. A tough life that does not interest the Chinese, thus the nomadic culture is the Tibetan culture that stands the best chance of survival. One year, though, the Chinese ordered the nomads to let the sheep remain in one area, while the Tibetans had from olden times moved them from pasture to pasture, over large distances, in one year. The order of the Chinese resulted in overuse of the pasture, and starvation of the sheep. It took the nomads many years to get the yield of the pastureland back to normal.

The life of the Tibetans is in concordance with nature, which further is in concordance with their Buddhist philosophy of mutual dependence of the living and non-living entities.

The tough climate in the highlands can be brutal. In the winter of 1995 ferocious snowstorms raged in Eastern Tibet – the worst in a hundred years. With heavy snowfalls of snow five meters deep and temperatures down to -45°C plus wind chill equals -90°C. Several hundred nomads froze to death, ten thousands turned snow blind, and 200,000 nomads lost their total income. In the districts of Kham and Amdo more than 500,000 yak and sheep froze to death or died from hunger. When the snow melted in the spring, it revealed a completely destroyed pastureland: The roots of grass and plants had died or been eaten away by insects.

To survive as nomads, one family needs ten sheep and four yaks as a minimum for existence. The whole nomad culture was at stake, ten thousand nomads moved to the towns and ended up as beggars.

What does a yak mean to the nomad?

Everything:

The butter is used in a nourishing tea, for butter lamps and to shape religious sculptures for the Tibetan New Year celebrations.

The cheese is used as dried snacks or in cooked food,

The fat is stored in hides and used for cooking and frying,

The milk is extremely nourishing, and is used for yoghurt, butter and cheese.

The meat tastes better than beef, is used in cooking and as dried snacks.

The dung is dried – the only available fuel in the wood-bare highlands.

The wool and the leather are used for clothes, shoes, bags, tents and boats.

From *the bones*, utensils and jewellery are made.

The horns are used for making ornaments, knife handles and musical instruments.

The tail is popular as flycatchers and fans in Tibetan as well as in Indian temples.

The yak is strong, stubborn, persistent, willing, loves thin air and looks like a wandering heap of wool. The wool is so thick that the yak can sustain -40^{0}C – equivalent to a deep freeze. The male is 1.80-2.00 meters high and weighs 600-1000 kilos. The female weighs 230-250 kilos and is called *dri*. The Tibetans giggle when you say *yak* butter – it is *dri* butter.

A less stubborn and milder variety is *Dzo*: Yak-plus-ox. He can plough in the fields all day without tiring, while the yak gets fed up before lunch. *Dzo-mo* is the female, which yields more milk than the Dri. The Dzo is labour efficient for fourteen years, while the yak is efficient for ten years.

A caravan of yaks is a majestic sight, every animal with its own hand knitted head gear and a thick hand knitted saddle carpet, with colourful Tibetan auspicious symbols. The yak carries a big burden. When the snow in the highlands is too deep to find food, the yak waits till he finds a slope where he can roll down, bringing down the snow with him. He eats his way up where the grass has been laid bare – and rolls down again. When coming from lower country to a highland plateau with thin air and icy wind, the yak snorts with delight, jumps about like a kid goat while the burden falls of, before settling and jogging on at a maximum speed of 3 km. per hour.

China Strangles Tibet

One of the main threats for the Tibetan people, the culture and the environment, is the massive immigration of military and civilian Chinese, in 1999 7.5 million Chinese to 6 million Tibetans. In the capital Lhasa there were then two Chinese to every Tibetan. The Tibetans are on the periphery socially, economically, in education and in politics, and the rich Tibetan culture and traditions are endangered. The Tibetans can end up as a curious minority in China. *However* in 2002, 2003 and 2004 there have been yearly talks between high officials in the Chinese government and H.H. the Dalai Lama's representatives, with the result a new wind be blowing? Some of the Tibetan political prisoners have been released. H.H. the Dalai Lama is still optimist (September 2010), and says he hopes to return to Tibet with a Tibetan passport.

In June 2006 the new railway from China to Lhasa was opened. This has been quite an achievement over the mountain ranges, and has cost China forty times what they have otherwise used in Tibet. It is good for economy, for industry and mines, for import and export, and for tourism, but there is also the danger of a new wave of Chinese immigrants.

In this previously so peaceful country there are seventeen secret radar stations, fourteen military airfields, and nine missile bases in 2004.

The Chinese are lured to Tibet with higher wages, free loans, better education, and these are the Chinese who have no possibility of a job or a future in their own country. The Chinese, not only in administration, but also in all fields, occupy all the important posts. Whether a Tibetan teacher or handicraftsman is better qualified: a Chinese gets the job first, and at a higher wage.

Tseten fled to India when he was sixteen, and joined a Tibetan school. Tseten was a happy lad who thrived and did very well at school. His greatest wish was to study Tibetan medicine. But then – during his last year at school, I received a sad letter from Tseten, a letter of farewell. His mother, a widow, and his sister, who had a job, begged Tseten to return to Lhasa. As Tseten had fled to India, the Chinese threatened his mother and sister with loss of job and home, if Tseten did not return. So Tseten returned. That was the last I heard from him, six years ago.

The schools: In many schools the Tibetan language is not taught, and while education is free for the Chinese children, the Tibetans have to pay. In addition the parents must pay for the schoolbooks, and give presents to the Chinese teachers – money as well as food. There is quite a system of bribes, which will result in good or bad marks. The result is that very many parents cannot afford to let their children go to school. That is mainly why it is a goal for many Tibetan parents to smuggle their children out of Tibet, with the dangers entailed, for a Tibetan schooling in a Tibetan cultural environment in India or Nepal. This does not suit the Chinese. So they have threatened the parents to call their children back. If not, the rest of the family members would lose their jobs. Still, many parents withstand the threat; to them their children are the future of Tibet. And in the schools in exile they learn to read and write Tibetan, and English, and they learn about Tibetan culture and Tibetan Buddhism. The parents must also pay high bribes for the children to go to the university in Lhasa.

However, in the Kham district Tibet Foundation, London, has been allowed to establish schools, where the children get a free education and boarding, and learn Tibetan, Chinese and English. Tibet Foundation has also established a medical school, a hospital and elderly peoples' homes in the same area. The elderly people are given yaks, which gives them meat, dairy products, wool and dung for fuel. And what they do not need themselves is sold. The hospital is a good customer! In this way, the elderly people get enough money to finance their homes.

Jobs: You have to speak and read Chinese and pay bribes to get a job, even a receipt is in Chinese only. However, here a small change has started: The street names are now written in Tibetan as well as Chinese.

The Tibetan language has no big function in society – only privately.

In some villages there are on schools. For the Chinese there is not so much interest in building schools outside the towns – the farmers and the nomads have no status. The farms are only interesting if they are big enough. The Chinese do interfere with how the farming is done, though. China needs wheat, and the Tibetans were one year ordered to grow wheat instead of their traditional barley. Wheat however, gives a very poor yield in the Tibetan highland climate – and that year there was a widespread famine...

Not only does the capital Lhasa have more than two Chinese inhabitants to one Tibetan. The Chinese run 90% of all shops, restaurants and bars. Quite a monopoly! And in this the most holy city of Tibet, the Chinese run more than 1,800 brothels. There are brothels and Karaoke bars, casinos and shopping centres. The streets are swarming with beggars, prostitutes and people without jobs.

This monopoly is noticed all over Tibet, in all fields. Shops, factories, mines, forestry, tourism...

Religion: Religion is the most important part of every Tibetan's life and conduct... What the tourists see is purely cosmetic. In 1950 there were more than 6,000 monasteries in Tibet, with as much as 6-8,000 monks in several of them. In 1980 only thirteen were left. The Chinese destroyed the remaining monasteries, during the Cultural Revolution. At the beginning of the 1980's the Chinese allowed delegations from the exile government of the Dalai Lama to visit Tibet, as they thought they had by now totally destroyed religion. They were taken totally by surprise over the reception these delegations got from the Tibetans. At that time fifty to sixty monasteries had been partly or wholly reconstructed by Tibetans, who worked voluntarily and without pay for months. Now there are strong restrictions on reconstruction and repair and in fact there has been more fresh destructions. In 1997 only, 526 monasteries were destroyed in the province of Kham. The argument of the Chinese authorities was that the monasteries were part of a feudal system based on blind faith. "Thus we have taken effective steps to destroy thousands of monasteries in the region, and by that obliterated a reawakening of bad influence."

Gyalke, 30 years old was in1999 the eldest monk in the Pomda monastery. The Chinese distributed books with distorted views and Chinese propaganda, which the monks were forced to read for hours every day. Gyalke refused to read such books, as they contained false information about the Dalai Lama and the reincarnation process. The police stripped him naked and dragged him to the local police station for arrest. In the prison Gyalke was hit till he lost control of his urinary bladder, and hit with an electric baton that gave him mental problems.

Kyaga, 30 years old was arrested for having pasted up a poster: Free Tibet, and torn down an official Chinese sign which he threw into the ditch. He was sentenced to eleven years' imprisonment. He is released now, but still suffers from mental problems after torture and heavy beatings in the prison. The Chinese broke several of his ribs, and he had strong pains as one rib touched his kidney. (Source: Tibetan Centre for Human Rights & Democracy, Dharamsala)

Young monks and nuns are not allowed entrance to a monastery till they are 18 years old, and their fields of spiritual activities are limited. To practise or teach Buddhism – the roots must be cut off. In every monastery there is systematic indoctrination in Chinese politics. For the Tibetans, however, religion is life itself, and they will not be subdued. Again and again there are demonstrations and protests, headed by monks and nuns – as they have no families dependent on them. They are imprisoned, and many of them brutally tortured. In Norway everyone remembers the Tibetan monk Palden Gyatso, who had been imprisoned for 33 years. When he visited Norway in 2000, he demonstrated peacefully with Tibetans and sympathisers one day, during the visit of the Chinese president Zemin, and was pushed into a police car. This actually proved to be a great success: As a result of the wholehearted reactions from the Norwegians viewing this scene on the television, a door suddenly opened far into the government, and the media queued to interview Palden Gyatso. We all saw him on the news, where he told us about the torture he had suffered, showing his scars, his handcuffs and his toothless mouth, while his tears streamed. Many nuns and monks have died in prison, as a result of the torture.

Electrical instruments with needles, knives with saw teeth and lashes with knobs were used liberally. One third of the prisoners were women. They were raped, and electrical batons pushed up their vagina. These are only a few examples. Many commit suicide – a very drastic solution for a Buddhist who believes in reincarnation and karma. But even though they know what they risk, many continue to protest. Even after having been to prison. Many have been arrested with a picture of the Dalai Lama, or with the Tibetan flag, and this alone can result in prison for 3-17 years.

Gendhun Gyaltso, 18 years old monk, had hidden a drawing he made in the monastery: A mountain with a sun and a moon, and Tibetan text. The drawing was found, and in the icy winter cold he was dragged along the ground till the clothes were stripped off him. Then sentenced to four years' imprisonment.

When I met Nyima, 19 years old, in Dharamsala in 1990, she was distinctly marked by what she had been through. The past suffering was in her eyes. During a peaceful demonstration in Lhasa, Nyima was arrested and heavily beaten – she still suffered pain. The Chinese asked her to bear witness against two others, offering her release – but she refused. One of the two was later sentenced to death. The other got fifteen years. Nuns, who were in prison with Nyima, were hung by their arms and attacked by dogs. The mouth was forced open with knitting needles. They also had to strip naked and lie on the frozen ground. Nyima now lives in the US.

I met Zamlha, 25 years old in 1990. He still keeps in contact and has written a little book about what he had been through. When he was four years old, other children were denied playing with him, as his parents were "reactionary". They were deprived of all their belongings, sent to forced labour, and always had to wear dunce caps. As six years old, Zamlha wished to go to school, but with reactionary parents that was out of the question. Instead he had to work – emptying latrines. When he was ten years old, he was arrested for the first time, and heavily beaten about the kidneys. As thirteen years old, he was set to dig ditches for the sewage pipes. Carried heavy stones till he fainted, a stone fell on him and he broke five ribs.

Then he became a monk and started his underground work. Made and distributed posters, demonstrated, was imprisoned, escaped, was expelled, imprisoned, escaped once more. During the celebration of the Tibetan New Year in 1988 there was a major demonstration in Lhasa. It amounted to several, and the Chinese not only arrested hoards of people, but also began shooting with machine guns. A picture shows a shocked Zamlha behind a friend who got killed.

When I met him two years later in Dharamsala, he was still suffering from the after effects.

China has great confidence in its strong and growing economy. The Chinese know this also gives them political power, and that the West does not want to risk treading too much on their toes. When confronted with not showing respect for human rights, they only repudiate this by replying that we have no say in their interior rule. However, Tibet complied in all the criteria of UN as an independent state. The Tibetans still hope and trust there will be a positive change through dialogue and peaceful means.

New Thumbscrew in Tibet:

Report dated July 2000 from Kelsang Namgyal, now resident in Sweden. He then returned to visit Tibet:

"The first person I met, was an old friend, a monk. I was overjoyed to see him, but in my hotel room, the truth was spoken, about the new harsh rule of the Chinese in Tibet. 'This is a new cultural revolution', he told me in a low voice. 'Some years ago the Chinese decided that the portrait of H.H. the Dalai Lama would not be allowed in schools, monasteries or in the homes of those working for the government.'

'Now however, they have denied every Tibetan the right to have a house altar, Buddha figures, pictures and the like in their homes. They invade the homes, throw it all out, and force the Tibetans to applaud while they burn everything, taking a film of the event. If you refuse to applaud, you are arrested.

'Hundreds of nuns and monks find they have to leave their monasteries, because, if they stay, their families will be threatened and molested. You are not allowed to burn incense in the temples, are not allowed to visit the monasteries, which normally is a daily routine. No one understands how bad the Chinese treat us,' my friend told me. 'I cannot understand how the Chinese can destroy an entire culture that has existed for more than a thousand years.'

"The next day I went to my village to visit my parents. Though they were so happy to see me again, they were very downhearted. 'There is a new cultural revolution going on in Tibet', my mother whispered, even though we were alone. 'The Chinese patrols have so far penetrated into our home three times. They removed the altar and took all our ritual things which we use daily. I don't want to live in this village any more; in fact I don't want to live any longer. The situation is desperate". Tears rolled down her cheeks.

Two days later I visited a nomadic district. Many of the nomads told me the same story. Then I visited a cousin in another village. As we drew near in our jeep, we saw the men and women of the village run out of it and up into the mountain, and we experienced a ghost village. Every house was locked and not a soul to be seen. After some time the villagers returned, one by one. They realised that this time it was not the Chinese patrols, but visitors who had arrived. Everyone gathered in the house of my cousin, some with serious expressions, others laughing nervously.

The previous week the Chinese had been there, searched through every single house, removed all the house altars and the pictures of Dalai Lama and Karmapa Lama, the latter being the young and leading lama, who fled to Tibet in the spring 2000, 14 years old. One of the elders of the village said with tears in his eyes: "We Tibetans live with the threat of having our whole culture being eradicated, and still people do not know how we suffer. Please tell H.H. the Dalai Lama and everyone living outside Tibet about the unhappy state of Tibet today."

With the new contact between the Chinese and the exile Tibetan governments, let us hope and pray that the miserable picture described above, will soon be history!

The soul of the Tibetan: Have you ever experienced the Tibetan smile? It arises from deep within, spreads, lights through the whole face – a smile of joy, compassion, humanity, and knowledge of a deep reality – which gives you a shock of deep, experiencing joy.

I have already mentioned Dr. Tenzin Choedrak. However, there is more to his story. He was so severely tortured that a Chinese doctor had to warn – "We must pause now, or he will die from this." In the prison camp where he had to eat his own clothes and his leather belt to survive, he caught deadly dysentery He survived, through heat creating tum-mo meditation and millions of mantras. Some years ago he was interviewed by an American psychiatrist in the USA – a leading expert on post-war traumas of the veterans from the war in Vietnam. But never had he experienced such a "patient". There was not the least trace of psychical damage, no bitterness, no traumas. What he did have, to the fullest extent, was the Tibetan smile – the smile of the soul. Filled with warmth and bubbling humour.

The Tibetan boys who came to Norway in 1964, 10 to 18 years old, had sad experiences behind them. But the smiles radiated, from deep within.

The technological and scientific culture of the West has spread worldwide. The inner culture of the Tibetans also ought to spread worldwide. We cannot afford to lose a culture that has the key to the smile of the soul.

The Dalai Lama was young when he fled to India, but from that very moment he was utterly aware that it would be him and the 120,000 Tibetans who went into exile with him, who would preserve the rich Tibetan culture in all its fields. With utter stamina he has created the base to preserve all parts of the culture in exile – apart from the nomadic

The Wind horse: Prayers are carried with the wind. Stands also for strength, speed, obedience and perseverance.

culture, which is bound to the mountain areas of the Himalayas.

In exile not only have the many facets of the culture been preserved, they have also spread to the whole world; Tibetan Buddhist philosophy, the philosophy of non-violence, their medicine, their carpet industry and other handicrafts, drama and music – to mention a few. Exile Tibet is a vigorous mini-Tibet that grows against the wind. With modern education and a modern democracy as new facets, the people can develop Tibet into a modern land of peace, with autonomy. This is the dream of the Dalai Lama.

One of the many thoughts of the Dalai Lama is that he thinks of Western science and the philosophy of the East fusing to create a really whole and developed human existence in our modern world. Only in this way can we be strengthened in our situation today, and become whole.

The statistic materials have the following sources: *Tibet Foundation, Tibetan Centre for Human Rights and Democracy, – Department of Information & International Relations, Central Tibetan Administration.*

Appendix II

Some Tibetan Medicine Clinics in the USA

California :

Santa Cruz: Dr. Yangdron Kalsang, Five Branches Institute, 200 Seventh Avenue, suite 115, Santa Cruz, CA 95062
Phone: (831) 476-9424, Fax (831) 476-8928

Menlo Park: 841 El Camino Road, Menlo Park, CA 94025
Tisch Way; Ste. 605,

San Josè: CA 95128, Phone (408) 260-0208
e-mail: tcm@fivebranches.edu

San Francisco: Tibetan Wellness & Healing Center, 1249-46th Avenue, San Francisco, CA 94122
Phone: (415) 681-1643, (831) 239-2035
e-mail: tibetanhealth2003@yahoo.com

San Diego: Dr. Lobsang Dhondup, Tibetan Healing Center, 4115 Third Avenue, San Diego, CA 92103
Phone: (619) 325-0992
e-mail: sondrab@tibetanacademy.com

Massachusetts:

Dr. Sowa Rigpa, Yuthog Center for Natural Health Care, Springfield, Massachusetts, Phone: (413) 734-1341
e-mail: bluemedbuddha@yahoo.com

New York:

Dr. Marcha Woolf, Alternative Resources Limited/Menla Tibetan Institute, 101 West 23 Street # 158, New York, NY 10011, Phone/fax: (212) 741-2727

NY 10011, Phone/fax: (212) 741-2727

Dr. Tenzin Namgyal, 37-31 Crescent Street # 36, L.I.C. NY 11101, Phone: (212) 769-6485

Dr. Choeying Phuntsok, Meridian Medical Group 102 E. 30th Street, NY 10016, Phone: (212) 683-1221/ (718) 446-4580, e-mail: c_phuntsok@yahoo.com

Wisconsin:
Medicine Buddha Healing Center, 6595 Clyde Road, Spring Green, WI 53588-8080, Phone: (608) 583-4241, Fax (608)583-4243, e-mail: mbhc@mhtc.net, Web: www.medicinebuddhahealing.org

Washington:
Orcas Island (San Juan Islands, northwest of Seattle): Dr. Thubten Lekshe, Tanaduk Clinic of Tibetan Medicine, P.O. Box 1886, 123 North Beach Road, Eastsound, WA 98245, Phone: (360)376-8272 e-mail: amchi@tibetandoctors.com

Men-Tsee-Khang (Tibetan Medical & Astro. Institute) Clinics in India, Sikkim and Nepal:

1. Chopheling Tibetan Settlement, P.O. Miao, Distt. Changlang, Arunachal - 792 122. Tel.: 03807-222588.

2. Branch Clinic, New Bazar Lane, P.O & Distt. Tawang, Arunachal - 790 104. Tel.: 03782-222588.

3. P.O. Tindolong/Tezu, Distt. Lohit, Arunachal - 792 001. Tel.: 03804-222585.

4. Siddharth Vihar, Buddhist Cultural Society, Itanagar, Arunachal - 791 111.

Tel.: 0360-2291539.

5. P.O. Tuting, Distt. Upper Siang, Arunachal - 792 061. Tel.: 03799-222852.

6. P.O. Kamleshwarpur/Mainpat, Distt. Sarguja, Chattisgarh - 497 127. Tel.: 07834-263246.

7. 13, Jaipur Estate, East Nizamuddin, New Delhi - 110 013. Tel.: 011-24356503.

8. New Camp, House No. A-32, Majnu-Ka-Tilla, Delhi - 110 054. Tel.: 011-23817432/23816306.

9. Ladakh Buddhist Vihar, Near (ISBT) Bela Road, Delhi - 110 004. Tel.: 011-23924592.

10. 21 Adarsh Complex, Asian House, Near Swastik Cross Road, Navrangpura, Ahemdabad, Gujarat - 380 009. Tel.: 079-30460036/3046003.

11. 6/7, Siddharth Shopping Centre, Summer Club Road, Jamnagar, Gujarat - 361 005. Tel.: 0288-2671122.

12. Branch Clinic, P.O. McLeod Ganj/Dharamsala, Distt. Kangra, Himachal - 176 219. Tel.: 01892-221484.

13. Gangchen Kyishong, P.O. Dharamsala, Distt. Kangra, Himachal - 176 215. Tel.: 1892-223222/307068/307069.

14. Block No. 18/A, No. 96/97, Main Road, Kusumpti, Shimla - 171 009. Tel.: 0177-2624504.

15. Middle Bakrota, P.O. Dalhousie, Distt. Chamba, Himachal - 176 304. Tel.: 01899-240814.

16. P.O. Bhuppur/Paonta Sahib, Distt. Sirmour,

Himachal Pradesh - 173 025. Tel.: 01704-223547.

17. Near Gunpa Road, P.O. Manali, Distt: Kullu, Himachal Pradesh - 175 131. Tel.: 01902-251189.

18. P.O. Bir, Distt. Kangra, Himachal Pradesh - 176 077. Tel.: 01894-268370.

19. Branch Clinic, P.O. Jispa, Tehsil: Keylong. Distt. Lahual/Spiti, Himachal - 175 132. Tel.: 01900-233205.

20. P.O. Choglamsar, Distt. Leh, Ladakh, Jammu & Kashmir - 194 101. Tel.: 01982-253566.

21. P.O. Bylakuppe, Distt. Mysore, Karnatake - 571 104. Tel.: 08223-254231.

22. Branch Clinic Camp # 3, P.O. Tibetan Colony Mundgod, Distt. North Kannada, Karnataka - 581 411. Tel.: 08301-245716.

23. P.O. Tibetan Colony, Kollegal, Distt. Chamrajnagar, Karnataka - 571 457. Tel.: 08225-273297.

24. P.O. Gurupura/Hunsur Taluk, Distt. Mysore, Karnataka - 571 188. Tel.: 08222-246071.

25. (Camp# 6) P.O. Tibetan Colony, Mundgod, Distt. North Kannada, Karnataka - 581 411. Tel.: 08301-245071.

26. City Apartment, Shop # 12, Plot No. 21, Sector 16, Kopar Kairanne, Navi Mumbai - 400 709. Tel.: 022-27540106.

27. Shree Malad Jain Yuvak Mandal Medical Centre, Mukta Bagh, Near Subway, Malad West, Mumbai - 400 064. Tel.: 022-65239654.

28. P.O. Pratapgarh, Tehsil: Arjuni/Morgaon,

Distt. Gondia, Maharastrata - 441 702.
Tel.: 07196-223024.

29. Near NCC Office, Lower Lachumiere, Shillong, Meghalaya - 793 001. Tel.: 0364-2227583.

30. Thubten Cheling Gonpa, Junebasi (East No. 3), Solo Khumbu, Nepal

31. Kailash Medical Astro. Society, 3/114, Dalko, P.O. Box No. 2823, Kathmandu, Nepal. Tel.: 00977-1-4251994/4248889.

32. Kailash Medical Astro. Society, 7(HA), 966/967, Maijubahal Chabahil, P.O. Box No. 2823, Kathmandu, Nepal. Tel.: 00677-1-4474025/4484869.

33. Kailash Medical Astro. Society, C7O Lekshedh Tsal Tibetan Day School, Post Box No. 417, Hiletar, Pokhara, Nepal. Tel.: 00977-61-535262.

34. Kailash Medical Astro. Society, Tashi Palkhiel Tibetan Settlement, Hyangja, Post Box No. 417, Pokhara, Nepal. Tel.: 00977-61-521702.

35. P.O. Mahendragada, Disttt. Gajapati, Orissa - 761 034. Tel.: 06816-257497.

36. Govt. QRS – VC½, Unit – I (In front of Chowdhury Market), Bhubaneshwar, Orissa - 751 009. Tel.: 0674-2530396.

37. Ragasha Building, Namnang Road, Gangtok, Sikkim - 737 101. Tel.: 03592-204219.

38. Kunpheling Tibetan Settlement, P.O. Ravangla, Distt. Namchi, South Sikkim - 737 139. Tel.: 03595-260614.

39. Dekyiling Tibetan Setlement, P.O. Kulhan, Distt. Dehra Dun, Uttarakhand - 248 001. Tel.: 0135-2607380.

40. 225, Rajpur Road, P.O. Rajpur, Distt. Dehra Dun, Uttarakhand - 248 009. Tel.: 0135-2735383.

41. HC-339, Ganga Nagar, Meerut City, Uttar Pradesh - 250 001. Tel.: 0121-4023025.

42. Rai Bahadur Compound, Relli Road, P.O. Kalimpong, Distt. Darjeeling, West Bengal - 734 301. Tel.: 03552-255153.

43. 26, H.D. Lama Road, P.O. Darjeeling, West Bengal - 734 101. Tel.: 0354-2254735.

44. Opp. Bhutan Power House, Gref Road, P.O. Jaigaon, Distt. Jalpaiguri, West Bengal - 736 182. Tel.: 03566-264067.

45. C/O Dapon/Rupon's Office, H:Q: Est. No. 22, C/O 56 A.P.O.

46. Sevoke Road, (Siliguri), P.O. Salugara–734318 Distt. Jalpaiguri, West Bengal - 734 008. Tel.: 0353-2590354.

47. 48/6A, P.C. Mitra Lane (Swiss Park), Tollygunge, Kolkata - 700 033. Tel.: 033-24241222/24248019.

48. C/O. Mrs. Nyima Lama Sharpa, Village: Khong Khola, P.O. Sonada, Distt. Darjeeling, West Bengal - 734 219.

49. Sorig Production Unit, Khotpura Road, Village Ganjbar, G.T. Road, Panipat, Haryana - 132 103. Tel.: 0180-6451217.

51. Branch Clinic at Manicipal Door No. 6-1.
    tp 4/B Padmarao Nagar,
    Behind Lakahimi Apartment,
    Secunderabad, Andhra Pradesh - 50002.

52. C/O Tabo Ancient Monastery,
    TEH: Spitt, VPO Tabo - 172 113.
    Distt. Lahaul Spitt. Himachal Pradesh

Appendix - III
Tibetan Doctors

(Who have contributed and guided the author in composition of this book.)

TENZIN CHOEDRAK (1924 - 2002). He is said to have been the most gifted Tibetan doctor in the last century. Educated and worked at Tibetan Medical Institute in Lhasa, he was imprisoned and tortured by the Chinese for seventeen years. He fled to Dharamsala in India in 1979, and was appointed senior personal physician to H.H. the Dalai Lama. The most complicated *Precious Pills,* the one with 185 ingredients, was mainly invented by him. It helps against modern poisons of our time, and this was used by him during Chernobyl nuclear diaster in Russia. He travelled worldwide to teach and cure. At home he taught and guided junior doctors and medical students about the theory and practice of Tibetan medicine.

DAWA (1958-). Educated at Men-Tsee- Khang in Lhasa he was part of the research committee of traditional Tibetan medicine. He joined the school of Botanical Art of the Central Health Department of China in 1980, and became an expert on drawing medicinal plants, which later resulted in *A Clear Mirror of Medicinal Plants.* In 1988 he left for India, and became head of the Materia Medica Department. He became General Secretary of Men Tsee Khang in 2004, and then Director in 2005. Currently, he is a special advisor to the cultural departments of Men-Tsee-Khang.

Tsee-Khang.

YESHI DONDEN (1929-). He was educated in Tibetan Medicine in Lhasa, Tibet. He remained for more than twenty years the personal physician of H.H. the Dalai Lama in Dharamsala, India, where he also founded a Tibetan Medical Center.

PEMA DORJEE. He qualified at Men-Tsee-Khang in 1974. He runs several Tibetan clinics in India and Nepal. He is General Secretary at Men-Tse-Khang in Dharamsala and is one of H.H. the Dalai Lama's private physicians. He has written two books and several articles on Tibetan medicine and attended many conferences and seminars.

TENZIN NAMDUL (1972-). He graduated in 1996 and then worked in the research and development department. Currently he is working as clinical researcher at Men-Tsee-Khang in Dharamsala.

DORJEE RAPTEN NESHAR. He fled to India in 1969, and started his medical study in 1982. He is Chief Medical Officer at Tibetan Medical Centre, Bangalore and was awarded Gold Medal from the Indian Board of Alternative medicine for his research cancer and diabetes. He is a widely travelled man in pursuance to his medical duty to Europe, USA, Japan and South Korea.

THOKMAY PALJOR (1960-). He worked at the branch clinic in Lhadak for five years. Back in Dharamsala he taught Tibetan medicine. He has translated the *Four Tantras* together with Dr. Sonam Dolma. He is currently head of translation department at Dharmasala. He has given medical consultations and presentation in several European countries and Japan.

NAMGYAL QUSAR (1961-). He served in Men-Tsee-Khang's research and development department for seven years, and discovered the properties of several herbal medicines.

He is the main project initiator and project designer on various clinical research studies. He held consultations and lectures in USA and many countries in Europe. Currently he is the chief editor of *Tibetan Medicine and Astrology Journal* and runs his own clinic in Sidhpur.

LOBSANG RAPGAY. He is a Tibetan Buddhist monk, who has a Ph.D. from Visva Bharti University, Shanti Niketan, West Bengal, India, in Tibetan Medicine and Buddhist Psychology. He runs a clinic in New Delhi and works closely with the Department of Behavioural Medicine, Beth Israel Hospital and Harvard Medical School, California, USA. He is also a Research Associate of the New York Heart Research Foundation, and an elected member of the Council for International Association of Traditional Asian Medicine.

TSEWANG TAMDIN. He is the director of the Tibetan Medical and Astro Institute (*Men-Tsee-Khang*) in New Delhi, and has for many years alternated with Dr. Pema Dorjee as visiting doctor to London, through Tibet Foundation. They are both personal physicians to HH the Dalai Lama.

NAMGYAL TENZIN (1972-). He graduated from Men-Tsee-Khang in 1993 and worked at the Research Department till 1998. He has translated an English-Tibetan Medical Dictionary and was coordinator for the research on Type 2 diabetes, in collaboration with All India Medical Sciences (AIIMS), New Delhi. At present he runs his private clinic in New York.

LOBSANG TSULTRIM TSONA. After finishing Primary School in 1981, he qualified for Men-Tsee-Khang in 1986. During his studies, he worked for two years as an apprentice to his father, a specialists in formulating herbal pills. He has lectured in many countries including the Netherlands, Germany, Switzerland, Norway, France, Poland, the Czech Republic, Canada and Japan. In 1994 he studied Western medicine at AIIMS, New Delhi. He has also Worked with Dutch Foundation for Tibetan Medicine and since 2003 he is runing his own practice at Ede in the Netherlands.

LOBSANG WANGYAL (1922 - 2003). He fled from Tibet in 1983, after spending seven years in prison. Together with Dr. Choedrak he has helped to save the Tibetan medical tantras. In Dharamsala he was appointed junior personal physician to H.H. the Dalai Lama. Dr. Wangyal has travelled as a doctor to most of the countries in Europe, to USA, to Australia, and to Asia, (especially India, Nepal, Mongolia, Japan and South Korea).

BIBLIOGRAPHY

Avedon, John F.

1985 : *In Exile from the Land of Snows,* Wisdom Publications

Bradly, Tamdin Sither

2000 : *Principles of Tibetan Medicine,* Thorsons Publications

Clifford, Terri

1984 : *Tibetan Buddhist Medicine and Psychiatry: The Diamond Healing,* The Aquarian Press

Dawa, Sonam

2000 : *A Clear Mirror of Tibetan Medicinal Plants,* Associazione Tibet Domani, Roma Ostiense, Italia

Dalai Lama, the H.H.

1983 : *My Land My People*

1997 : *The Book of Wisdom,* Rider

1999 : *Ancient Wisdom, Modern World*

Dalai Lama, the H.H. with Galen Rowell

1990 : *My Tibet*

1991 : *The Dalai Lama and Others MindScience,* Wisdom Publications

Donden Yeshi

1986 : *Health through Balance,* Snow Lion Publications

2000 : *Healing from the Source,* Snow Lion Publications

Goldstein and Beall
Nomads of Western Tibet, Serinida

Gyatso Palden
1999 : *Fire under the Snow,* Harvill Press

Hallvard Kare Kulîy
1988 : *Tibetan Rugs,* White Orchid Books

Journal of the Tibetan Medical & Astro Institutes, *Man-r Tsis*
1995 : Vol. I, No. 1 & 2
1996 : Vol. II, No. 1

Norbu, Thubten J. and H. Harrer
1987 : *Tibet is My Country*

Rapgay, Lobsang
Tibetan Therapeutic Massage, Own publishing

Ricard, Matthieu and J.F. Revel
1999 : *The Monk and the Philosopher,* Thorsons Publications

Rinpoche, Sogyal
1992 : *Tibetan Book of Living & Dying,* Harper Collins
1994 : *Meditation - A Little Book of Wisdom*
1995 : *Glimpse after Glimpse,* Random House

Tsarong, T. J.
1986 : *Handbook of Traditional Tibetan Drugs,* Tibetan Medical Publications

Tibetan Medicine Series, Library of Tibetan Works and Archives
1980 : No. 1 and No. 3
1981 : No. 2
1985 : No. 2 and No. 9
1988 : No. 11
1989 : No. 12

Weber, Renè
1999 : *Dialogue with Scientists and Sages*

INDEX

T